THE AUTONOMOUS FREELANCER

THE AUTONOMOUS FREELANCER

ON YOUR OWN TERMS
IN YOUR OWN TIME
AT YOUR OWN RATE

DOMINIC KENT

Copyright © 2023 by Dominic Kent

All rights reserved. No part of this book may be used or reproduced in any manner without written permission from the publisher, except in the context of reviews.

All trademarks are the property of their respective companies.

Cover and Interior Design: jessica@dezinermama.com

ISBN: 979-8-374301403

1 2 3 4 5 6 7 8 9 10

CONTENTS

Foreword 1

About This Book 3

About The Author 7

Chapter 1
The Benefits of Being an Autonomous Freelancer 9

Chapter 2
Dispelling Freelance Myths 21

Chapter 3
Setting Yourself Up for Freelance Autonomy 45

Chapter 4
How to Make Work Come to You 81

Chapter 5
How to Find Your Niche in a Noisy Online World 91

Chapter 6
How to Price Work With Autonomy in Mind 111

Chapter 7
How to Put Getting Paid on Autopilot 133

Chapter 8
How to Diversify Income Without Reinventing the Wheel 147

How to Become an Autonomous Freelancer Right Now 163

Tools and Resources 165

FOREWORD

by Dom Black, Research Director at Cavell Group.
(Also, a really nice client.)

Reading your last Twitter thread, I thought you're probably close to the stage of putting out your first book on your learnings of launching a successful freelance business.

I've not looked into it, and am sure there are loads similar, but I think there is definitely a book on what you've achieved so far. At least somewhere other than Twitter for people to learn from your experience.

ABOUT THIS BOOK

First and foremost, thank you for purchasing, borrowing, or stealing this book. It means a great deal that you put your trust in me to help you take your freelance career to the next level.

I am writing this book with three types of people in mind. The heaviest focus is on the third type. My hope is that by the time you've read this book, you'll be in a position where you classify yourself as that third type and are ready to kick on and take your freelance career to the next level.

The types of people I am writing this book for are:

- **The beginner freelancer**: you excel in a discipline and are exploring the possibility of doing more and getting paid for it. We don't dwell on this stage for long as hopefully the title of this book has attracted mostly the second and third types of people.
- **The freelancer**: you probably work full-time and use freelancing to supplement your income. Deep down, you would love freelancing to be your main source of income.

- **The full-time freelancer:** you depend on freelance work for the majority of your income. You have a portfolio (although we'll get onto those later), an online presence, and several contracts in play at any one time.

If you rolled your eyes at beginner freelancer or think you're nowhere near ready to take your freelance full-time, don't worry.

This book doesn't dwell on basic working life items like getting a laptop or making sure you have good internet. Neither does it ask you to make a huge commitment by subscribing to a yearly platform where you may or may not find work.

(Can you tell I've read some bad books on freelancing?)

My aim for this book is to provide clear advice and actionable steps so you can take your freelance career to the next level.

What is the next level?

The next level will be different for each of you reading this book.

But the goal is always autonomy.

What does autonomy mean for a freelancer?

In the simplest form, working on your own terms. In your own time. And on what you like. You are self-governed and work becomes a flow state.

Freelance autonomy is a goal that a huge portion of freelancers never achieve.

I have. And with the help of other high-performing freelancers, this book is dedicated to moving you forward.

So, your next level might be getting some freelance writing work. I'm confident you'll achieve this by the time you've finished reading this book.

You might do some freelance writing as a side gig and be wondering how to turn this into a more lucrative platform. Or even a full-time platform. I was this exact person. After I started writing £100 posts for an industry publication, I wanted more. More writing gigs and more money for doing a good job of them.

So, your next level would be establishing yourself as a genuine freelance writer. You want to be known in your area and be approached for work rather than having to seek it out or spend hours on applications you're pessimistic about.

You might be a full-time freelance writer. Full-time freelance is a weird phrase, isn't it? For a while, I wondered how making the transition from full-time employed with a part-time freelance gig would go. About three days in, I loved it. Five years later, I love it even more. I have a great set of clients, I get paid great money, and my time is mine. I work on my own schedule, in my own office (which is often a beach cafe), and say no to whoever the hell I like.

Your next level might be earning more without doing more work. It might be finding better clients. It might be enjoying your work more. After all, if you're going to spend over 75,000 hours of your life working, you want to enjoy it.

So, strap in and sit tight. Take out a notebook, load up your note-taking software, or open the note section of your phone, and get ready for....

I wish I could say you're in for a rollercoaster ride but that would be lying. (Unless you plan to take this book on a rollercoaster.) If so, please send me a photo on Twitter. I'm @DomKent

But do get ready to take notes. Everything I am going to reference in this book is designed to help you take your freelance career to the next level.

You might want to put this book down and action something immediately. There's a bunch of people you should follow on Twitter. There are a few blog posts you should read. (Don't save them to Pocket; you'll never read them.) There are one or two things you should sign up to.

Let's go.

ABOUT THE AUTHOR

While you probably don't care about me, I thought it important to provide you with evidence that you're in good hands.

My current pinned tweet does a good job of explaining why I'm qualified to write this book:

"Today is my 4-yr freelancing birthday.

In that time, I've:

- Worked 4-day weeks
- Written 250 articles
- Delivered 30,000 leads
- Made $700,000 for myself
- Accumulated 5m+ pageviews
- Generated $5m+ client revenue"

But do you know what the best part is?

I've done it all my way.

For the entirety of my freelance career, everything I've worked on has been on my own terms.

So that's me. Sure, people earn more than me. Or work less than me. But I'm mighty happy.

And that's because I'm an autonomous freelancer.

If you can't tell, I'm a freelance writer/marketer. Because of this, most of my first-hand examples come from a writing/marketing perspective. Don't let that put you off if you're a developer, designer, or anything else you've become freelance in. Everything in this book can be applied in any freelance scenario. At the end of the day, it's just doing work for someone (or yourself).

Oh, one more thing. I hate spelling mistakes. If you find one in this book, please tweet me @DomKent and I'll get it changed.

CHAPTER I

THE BENEFITS OF BEING AN AUTONOMOUS FREELANCER

This is probably the most important chapter of this book. That's why I'm including it at the beginning.

> "Allowing autonomy in work settings supports team members in finding the optimum productivity outputs to improve the company's overall health."
>
> —Unnamed author at Siemens Smart Infrastructure for Forbes

In Drive, by Daniel H. Pink, he describes **autonomy** as being self-directed, **mastery** as improving your skills, and **purpose** as connecting to something bigger than yourself.

While I agree with all of these, it's autonomy that often triggers mastery and purpose. So mastery and purpose become obvious benefits of autonomy.

You might achieve mastery in a skill or service without being a freelancer. And that's helping a wider purpose of the company you work for. But it's not personal purpose. It's personal autonomy, mastery, and purpose we strive for in this book.

So, here's how this chapter is going to work…

First up, I'm going to write (in one take) how happy I am as an autonomous freelancer.

Secondly, I'm going to add the thoughts of other autonomous freelancers in their own words.

Finally, I'm going to dispel some myths I've heard time and again since deciding to go full-time freelance.

Since going freelance (and becoming autonomous), I've never been happier

All my career, I'd been very good at my job. Until one day I was doing something that I didn't really enjoy. And at a company where I didn't agree with its approach to working.

This made me less of an achiever and more of a tagger along. I felt uncomfortable. I felt like I was failing. I didn't feel like I was contributing much. Then one day, my position didn't need to exist anymore. And it was probably the right call.

It's not all doom and gloom. I got another job with the same pay and a better chance at commission. I enjoyed my work immensely and loved the people I worked with.

So, why did I pack this all in and go full-time freelance? Because I saw the long-term benefits staring me in the face.

While working full-time at this point in my career, I'd started (by accident) writing for an industry newspaper. There was an advert calling for contributors to a guest blog competition. I entered and I like to say I came fourth. (Only the top three were announced.)

After inquiring if I could write some more, I had my first taste of working for someone outside of my full-time employer. Every other Saturday, I'd write an opinion-based 1,000-word article in my outdoor office for £100. It was all rather pleasant. An extra £200 would sit nicely in my house fund. There really was no downside.

Back in the old days (2017) when people relied on email and phone for communication, very few people were writing about the likes of Slack and Microsoft Teams. Luckily (and I use this term through gritted teeth), I happened to be one of them. This is what kickstarted my genuine freelancing career.

I still have the message that Meredith Schulz, then VP of Marketing at Mio, sent me in June 2018:

"Hi Dominic,

I saw that you're available for contracting, and after previously reading several of your articles in UC Today, I thought you might be interested in helping write and/or edit & lead a content publication that our startup, https://m.io is launching. If you are the least bit interested I'd love to set up a time to speak further."

It was this message that was to change my life. I know that sounds dramatic. But it really was. Some people become freelancers and don't change anything at all. And that's fine.

But the appeal of not working 9-5, not visiting customers and staying overnight, not reporting to a boss, not completing endless paperwork because it's the process, and not sitting at my desk (or any desk), lit up my eyes like nothing before.

An average day in my life, today, is based on a process I call micro-rewarding. It's dead simple and it's displayed on the BuzzSumo Wellbeing Wall:

"Over time, I realized that I was most motivated (therefore most productive) when there was something to look forward to. I call it micro-rewarding. I've scaled this down to an hourly basis. At the end of each hour, as long as I've hit my goals, I reward myself by upping the stake as the day goes on."

Louise Linehan, Senior Content Manager at BuzzSumo, asked me to write this after I told her how I work when I met her at brightonSEO, Europe's biggest SEO conference.

As we were chatting, I recalled a tweet where I tracked everything I did in the day and ranked my work-life balance.

Here's the thread:

Today I'm trialing working in 1 hour sprints with a reward at the end of each hour. Follow this thread if you're interested in my progress.

| HOUR 1 | Task a: Checked all chats & emails.
Task b: Added 2 outreach quotes to blog
    post in progress
Task c: 500 words of whitepaper copy
Reward: made lattes.
Productivity: 10 | Work life balance: 10 |

| HOUR 2 | Task a: 1,000 words of whitepaper copy
Task b: design notes for my first 1,500 words
Reward: walk the dogs on the beach.
Productivity: 10 | Work life balance: 10 |

| HOUR 3 | Task a: checked chats & email again
Task b: added outreach quote to blog post
Task c: invoicing and reminders
Task d: 500 words of whitepaper copy
Reward: lunch with girlfriend
Productivity: 8 | Work life balance: 10 |

| HOUR 4 | Task a: sourced author for guest post.
Task b: 500 words of whitepaper copy.
Task c: design notes (including a hand drawn matrix)
    for my latest 1,000 words.
Reward: 12 holes of golf
Productivity: 8 | Work life balance: 10 |

| HOUR 5 | Task a: review and edit blog post from one of my
fave writers. This doesn't even feel like work.
Task b: chats/ emails before ending my day.
Reward: finished "early".
Productivity: 10 | Work life balance: 10 |

On this particular day, I worked five hours.

I made £2,750 ($3,350) that day. I also went to the beach and played golf and finished before 4pm.

In fact, sometimes I work *on* the beach. Sounds impractical but there are plenty of beach cafes with sufficient Wi-Fi to look after what you need.

Oh, but I have to pay for something? Two lattes is a small price to work somewhere that makes me smile and be productive. After all, it used to cost me £400 per month just to get to my office in London. I'd rather pay a local business.

To emphasize this point, I've written this book exclusively in cafes, pubs, and breweries. I figured removing myself from my usual setting would be a productivity trigger. Sure, it came with an expense—but I got value in the added inspiration and productivity.

I can count on one hand the number of bad days I've had since going full-time freelance...

- Google de-indexed all my client's blog posts by mistake and I had a very nervy few days thinking it was all my fault. (Would've happened whether freelance or in-house.)
- One or two days when the dread set in that I didn't have enough work for the rest of the year. I'm going through this process right now. The reality is that I have three very likely and very well-paid gigs coming in for the next six months and I've built a buffer through my product's previous work. *
- One or two days when I woke up feeling so ill that I couldn't work (and therefore earn no money). See previous point about building up a buffer; more on this later in the book.

*Since writing this section, all three gigs came in.

To summarize the benefits of becoming an autonomous freelancer, I can work on whatever I want, at the price I set, in whatever way I want.

Sure, I do work in my home office sometimes. I'm not a digital nomad—though freelancing opens that door—and I'm not rich enough to retire. But I absolutely love what I do *because of the way I get to do it.*

Sometimes it is the simple things. If I'm writing a whitepaper for an enterprise client, they're paying good money. But does that mean I adopt a corporate approach and rent office space for a few days?

Hell no.

I turn up my music and get my head down. Office life might be for you. And that's okay. The moral of the autonomous freelancer story is:

On your own terms. In your own time. At your own rate.

But enough about me…

What other autonomous freelancers are saying

Simon Hayhust, Hayhurst Consultancy:

"I used to work for a B2B market research agency until January 2021 when I went independent and have never looked back. I love the life I lead these days, and though at times I work much longer hours, the benefits of going solo easily outweigh those of working for someone else."

I countered Simon on this because I thought it sounded negative. The whole point is to work better, not longer, right? I literally said:

"I think the element of working much longer hours sometimes goes against the theme of what I'm working on."

I wasn't going to include this response until he set my mind at ease.

"Ha! I think, in fairness, my point is that sometimes working longer hours is now *my* choice. And if I do have to work over a weekend, I know that when I send the invoice out, I get to keep all the income. My working hours these days are much lumpier than they were when I worked full-time in business. Sometimes that works in my favor. Yesterday, for example, I was able to watch a fair chunk of the India vs England cricket on TV without a smidgeon of guilt. Even though I sometimes work over a weekend or while we are away on holiday, I would say overall I am probably working 20% fewer hours. I definitely wouldn't want to return to working for anyone else."

Maya Middlemiss, freelance commercial writer and host of the Future is Freelance podcast:

"One upside people don't always appreciate is the antifragility of freelancing, at a time of global uncertainty. Freelancers are used to change (and to seeing it coming), to managing their own careers and professional development, and are continually hustling*. Losing a key client may be a big blow but it rarely represents 100% of your income, unlike a layoff from an employed position, and you're probably streets ahead on personal branding/business development in many cases."

*Hustling is a term that gets confused often. I don't think Maya meant (and nor do I endorse) hustle culture that triggers burnout and means you're working 7 days a week from 7 til 7. But hustling to ensure you have a steady set of clients, a personal brand, and a rock-solid portfolio are excellent freelance traits to have.

I hadn't thought about this until Maya mentioned it. It sure is easy to get comfortable when working full-time. And again, that's okay. I have no issue with people who choose not to freelance.

But the recent news (mid-2022) of startup layoffs and enterprise hiring freezes shows that even the greatest full-time talent isn't safe forever.

Freelancers do have the edge when it comes to reacting to and preparing for such circumstances.

Amna Aslam, freelance content writer:
"I belong to a small city in an underdeveloped country. I used to curse my city that I cannot make a career in this city. But freelancing and remote work has changed my perspective. It was once my belief that I can only work with international companies if I moved out of my country. Now I am doing work on an international scale from my city. My career would have ended if there was no freelancing."

This resonates with me so much. And it's something I'd forgotten easily. I don't live in an underdeveloped area, but freelancing and remote work empowered me to work from anywhere.

So, I moved to the beach!

My story is completely different from Amna's so I thank her for opening my eyes to this.

Anna Burgess Yang, full-time account manager and part-time freelance writer:

"Full disclosure: I'm not a full-time freelancer. But I like to maintain around 2-3 regular freelance clients at any given time. I have a pretty unique experience: I was in Fintech for 15 years before I pivoted into content marketing and journalism. What I bring to the table as a freelancer is that I am my own subject matter expert. I have in-depth experience in both banking and technology.

I tried to take on freelance clients that weren't in my wheelhouse and it was a struggle. I didn't enjoy the work. To really make freelancing worthwhile (alongside working full-time and having 3 kids), I needed as much control as possible over what I was producing. And I found this by only taking on clients where I could be my own SME. Mostly FinTech or banking-adjacent.

Clients can give me a broad topic or theme and I can just write without a ton of research (other than sometimes including stats). It makes the work easy/enjoyable to write because I'm confident in the quality of the article. And the more I do, the easier it becomes to find new clients because I have a portfolio of very industry-specific work."

I love that Anna got in touch when I was looking for other people's personal benefits of freelance autonomy. One, because it reflects my career. I was the product guy at service providers for 10 years before going freelance. I also spent a lot of time juggling full-time work with freelance commitments. Two, all my clients are within my niche (more on that later) so I am not just a marketer for hire but someone with tons of experience in the domain. While the reliance on a full-time job reduces the autonomous element somewhat, it's a great way to showcase the choice element.

Linsey Knerl, freelance writer:
"I've been an autonomous freelancer for over 13 years, and it has been the only way to engineer the lifestyle I want. Homeschooling 6 happy, healthy kids, writing horror fiction on the side, homesteading, and only doing it because I can set my schedule, work on the road, and pick the clients that support my lifestyle values."

Now this is what I'm talking about. Engineer the lifestyle I want are the words I've been looking for to describe freelance autonomy.

I don't know Linsey personally, but I know that she does things her own way. Could you imagine how different Linsey's lifestyle would be if she was living paycheck to paycheck replicating a 9-5?

Sanketee Kher, freelance content writer:
"I'd stashed away 6 months' worth of salary in 2 months and was ready to take the plunge. I concentrated on creating a portfolio I could share with potential clients. I created a website with blog posts to showcase my work and wrote and designed an ebook to show people I can do serious work.

I barely sent 10-15 emails and DMs as my focus was my portfolio. I got a great response from almost every platform I signed up on. But, here's where the problem starts:

I was so focused on my fear of having dry spells, that I became more active with my applications, knowing that failure could be a few months away.

It was so easy to fixate on not making it as a freelancer that I forgot to take into account that this is something that could work out! So, I started to weed out poorly paying or difficult clients and replaced them with clients who worked in B2B SaaS. This meant I was doing work I genuinely enjoyed and it helped me manage my workload while I kept my focus on scaling up.

It hasn't been the smoothest journey managing my tasks and dealing with clients, but it definitely helped me learn way more than a traditional job could. And it also allows me to work at the pace I set, not the one that is forced on me.

While it's imperative to find your feet in this new journey, it's equally important to prepare for success because it might happen before you've even had the time to register it.

My recipe for happiness and freelance job satisfaction? Always, always, always stick to deadlines, plan out your month, and don't work for a price that doesn't make you happy because it's not worth it."

Sanketee's story touches on many points that resonate with a lot of freelancers. The saving money upfront aspect allows you to focus on attracting the right clients, saying no to poor clients, and genuinely scaling your business. If you can do this, you are one step on the way to autonomy, rather than relying on lots of little clients that sap your time and energy.

Preparing for success rather than failure is a tough mindset to crack but one I try to employ every day. The best example I can use is July 2022 when I had completed all my July and August tasks before the middle of July. This allowed me to do any of several things:

1. Start writing a book.
2. Get ahead on September work.
3. Dedicate time to filling up my future pipeline.
4. Have some guilt-free time off.

CHAPTER 2

DISPELLING FREELANCE MYTHS

My introduction to freelancing was a rather luxurious one. I was earning £55,000 base salary at 27 with the realistic potential to earn up to £40,000 commission based on my billable work.

It's the latter element that set me in good stead for never undercharging when I went full-time freelance. (More on pricing later.)

My dad, on the other hand, had been working self-employed for well over a decade after his business went bust. His experience of self-employed life was that sometimes he would get to his place of work and not have any work that day. Not only did he not *earn* any money but he *lost* money driving to find that out.

When I told my dad that I'd quit full-time employment, there were tears in his eyes. He thought I'd made the worst decision of my life. I like to think I've proved him wrong. Though that was never my motivation.

While I've always had my dad's voice at the back of my mind, I've only looked forward. But that's not to say others (including long-term freelancers) haven't circulated myths and presented their bad experiences as the only side to freelancing.

So this section is included to put your mind at ease.

Myth 1 - It's feast or famine!

I first heard this phrase when I was working as an editor for my longest-serving client. The writer I was chatting with asked if I had any more work for them.

> **Side note:** there is no shame in this. If you have time free, telling people is the best way to fill that time. There's this horrible stigma about looking weak because you might not have enough work to fill your week/month. My only advice in this situation is: *ignore it*.

I asked the writer what they had on and who they were working with. The previous month they'd had more work than ever. This month they only had half their normal workload. While I did provide them with some more articles to write, I also thought about how they got there in the first place.

The feast or famine scenario is one I've never wanted to end up in. Feast, sure. I often take on more work than I can complete (on paper).

This may seem alien to you. Lots of people think it's unethical. Some people think it leads to burnout. But there are several tactics to apply here.

It's part of this feast process that helps dispel the feast or famine myth.

In the simplest form, saying yes to more work makes up for potential work you *don't* get later on. It also gives you the opportunity to impress and secure more work from existing clients. That doesn't mean you have to work 15 hours a day to get it done, either. You can say yes now and set your delivery time. And we'll build on saving up more time for delivery instead of admin later in the book.

To dispel the feast or famine myth, we must dig into preparation, self-marketing, and setting ourselves up for autonomy. If you're forever waiting for clients to sign and creating proposals, you reduce your time for executing your skills and deliverables.

This is where personal branding, sharing your work, and sharing your success comes into play.

For context, I've never cold pitched a client. I've never sent a proposal more than five slides long and that took more than 30 minutes to create.

How?

By literally sharing my work and sharing my success. There is very little to unpack here. People hire me because of the quality of my work and the success it brings people that pay for it. And they know about this because I share it.

Here are some examples of what I share (on social media, in proposals, on my website, quite literally anywhere):

- A link to my latest article
- % Conversion of blog views to sign ups
- $$$ generated per article after 6 months
- Behind-the-scenes snippets when creating content
- Major client acquisitions attributed to content I created
- A graph showcasing results of my latest content refresh
- A highlights reel of featured snippets and #1 ranking posts on Google

Some of these need input from clients. Not every freelancer has access to analytics and sales figures.

Unless they ask.

Imposter syndrome or not, there's no excuse not to ask and no disbenefit from asking to see how your content is performing.

Now, I understand imposter syndrome. And sympathize immensely. In fact, until I went freelance and represented myself, I greatly suffered from imposter syndrome.

I was a twenty-something (looking more like 17) person in a suit tagging along to meetings with CEOs, technical experts, and extroverted "salespeople" who would quite literally fight over meeting room tables.

It's not that I didn't want to interject. It's more that I didn't have anything to add. I'd do my demo or present what I came to do; then carnage would ensue. So it was best to stay out of the way.

People preach "don't say anything if you don't have anything nice to say" and that "it's okay to be quiet in meetings". But in a corporate setting, try telling that to the dinosaurs who've always done it their way. You must *dominate the room* and make sure your customer speaks first.

You know, all those sales tactics that don't actually work. "Selling" my own services since becoming a freelancer has been much softer.

It's three quarters sharing what I do and one quarter making sure I want to work with a new client.

The latter part (making sure I want to work with them) is something I get asked a lot.

"How do you qualify your customers?"

I have three parts to my answer:

1. Am I going to enjoy working with this new client?
2. Are they going to help me grow as a freelancer?
3. Can they afford me?

I normally start with the end of this process by sending my services page over before we chat further. That's right... I show them my pricing before wasting half an hour on a discovery call.

You wouldn't believe (or maybe you would) how many people I've seen moan about time wasted either on pointless calls or waiting for prospects to not show up.

The remedy? Don't have them until your customer is committed. With over half my customers, I've never had a real-time call with them. With some, I've quite literally never spoken to them. There's a lot to be said for asynchronous work. The sooner you get comfortable with being genuinely independent and providing updates and proposals without explaining your work in a real-time call, the sooner you move towards autonomy.

And this plays a huge part in qualifications 1 and 2. If the customer isn't invested in working asynchronously, I'm not going to enjoy myself and I'm not going to grow as a freelancer.

Of course, the topics, audience, scope of work, and potential upside all play their part here too. If you aren't interested in the topic, it's not the right niche for you.

Myth 2 - Freelancing gives you all the time in the world

When I asked my Twitter followers for examples of freelance myths, Nikki Pilkington, a freelance writer, provided the following:

"Freelancers that work from home are available for lifts, phone calls, coffee, etc. at the drop of a hat."

Potentially due to films and books about freelance artists and photographers who swan all over the world, there's a huge assumption that freelancers don't actually spend any time working. And some of us, me included, enjoy the free time we manufacture so much that we share it on social media.

I like to balance this with tweets covering how blimen busy I am and when some projects take up much more time than anticipated. I've also spent a lot of time streamlining my processes.

From writing a blog post to chasing up invoices, I've made every step of my working week as efficient as it can be. The only variable is me.

Sure, if you charge a huge amount for your deliverables, you may not need to work as much as others. And to that, if the fee is justified, I say well done. But for others who're busy being busy, there are some simple tweaks you can make to your processes that help you become more efficient and get you a step closer to autonomy.

Automate tasks that don't need human intervention

You don't have to reinvent the wheel here and there's no need to spend any money to achieve this either.

If an invoice is overdue, I've heard of freelancers sending lengthy chaser emails that offer alternatives to payment, proposing new timelines, and all sorts. Even a call to check in on how your client's business is doing and see if there is a problem.

Now, this might seem friendly and ticks the boxes for relationship-building (sort of) but you need to get paid within the parameters you set (more on setting up contracts later).

If an invoice is overdue, make sure your invoicing software allows you to click "Send Reminder" with the click of a button.

I don't have many clients who don't pay me on time. But one regular client has a lot of long-winded processes to protect itself due to the number of invoices it pays. I don't mind getting paid a few days late as long as I do get paid. And I make sure of that by clicking the "Send Reminder" button on FreeAgent, my accounting software. In fact, I've now automated it so I don't even need to click it.

Nobody likes receiving reminders so it gets paid within hours. No detailed email. No call. No offer to defer payment.

And, sure, this might not work for every client. But these are the clients you need to think twice about if your goal is reaching autonomy. If you spend time on tasks that don't pay the bills, remove as many of those tasks as you can.

And, yes, that might mean being a bit ruthless at times. But you're not a charity. This is your livelihood, your career, and how you keep food on the table.

Outside of invoicing, you can schedule or automate social media posts. Free tools like Buffer, Typefully, Hypefury, and even Twitter's native scheduler help me always have tweets and LinkedIn posts ready to go. In general, I have one post per platform queued up at least two weeks before.

I don't go overboard here. This ensures I appear active on social media without me needing to be "always-on". But it also means my feeds aren't so full that I can post something spontaneous.

If you opt for Hypefury, you don't even need to think up a new tweet. The tool mines your best-performing tweets and suggests a time to post them.

Scheduling meetings is another big time suck. How many minutes do you think you lose per year due to meeting scheduling?

According to research by Charles Kergaravat, an experienced collaboration technology marketing leader, and Propeller Insight, over 31% of workers spend 30 minutes or more preparing for each meeting. On top of this, 36% spend over 15 minutes doing the "coordinating calendars dance" to schedule a time that works for everyone.

An easy way to reduce this insane amount of unbillable time is to automate meeting scheduling. You can use tools like Calendly for free to either send your calendar to potential meeting guests or let people book meetings directly from your website or content.

If you've optimized your site to drive organic traffic and convert it to a meeting, the ability for your potential customer to book a meeting removes several steps of email intros and finding a time slot.

With all this said, automation of tasks like these isn't a **must**. If you're effective in these areas already, bucking to peer pressure of "productivity" is often counterproductive. Andrew Brethauer, a B2B SaaS content marketer, asks "Is it odd to say ... nothing? I've started using Asana to keep track of 4 clients, but I've mostly just done everything in my head because the more programs and software you add, the more time you have to spend using it. I just keep things as simple as possible."

If the task or automation adds no value, ask yourself: what's the benefit?

Cut tasks that add no value

Here's everyone's favorite and least favorite topic: actually having meetings. We preach the few meetings mentality and work style but how many of us end up still having countless intro calls and catch-up meetings that don't result in new business or acceptance of a deliverable?

These, by the way, are the only genuine needs for meetings (in both my literal and figurative books).

Other than meetings, tasks like weekly updates don't need to exist when you're delivering short-term deliverables. For example, if you submit a blog post every week, there's no need to provide an update on the work you've done for that client. They can literally see the output.

If you're unsure of which tasks you can remove from your process, document your entire week next week.

On paper (or a weekly planner), note down every task you do in one column. Then, in the next column, write down the time you spent on this. In the final column, add a monetary amount to denote how much money that task and time earned you.

Halfway through your week, you'll discover there's a lot of zero-revenue work in your week. What comes next is a natural defense of your own actions. You started doing them through a conscious choice so your brain *will* defend itself.

Be ruthless with yourself. Commit to change. If these tasks don't offer any monetary value, they better have a bloody good reason for existence. Otherwise, remove them from your routine.

Find a routine that works for *you*

Lots of people ask me how I work so fast. The key isn't working fast. The key is working efficiently. And I do this by finding what works best for me at the time.

Sometimes, I finish working by 9am and feel no guilt whatsoever. Sometimes, I work until nearer midnight because I'm in the zone and/or I have committed to a ridiculous deadline (charge more for these!).

For the most part, the combination of enjoyable work that will help me grow as a freelancer, in my niche where I am a subject matter expert, and that is well-paid, is all I need to be efficient.

The work put in ahead of time (in the sales process) pays dividends when it comes to delivery.

I start every day at 7.30am. That's because I know that's when I'm most productive. If any customer asked me to work from 9-5, it would remove the most productive hour and a half of my day. When communicating this, it's always been enough to convince a customer to let me work in my own time.

(For the most part, customers don't care when you work.)

On the occasions where I'm working collaboratively with other team members, I factor in time for this, obviously. But I would never compromise my own productivity for the sake of "the norm".

And you shouldn't either. Find your routine, your motivation, or whatever makes you most productive.

You probably won't end up like those freelance artists in the films. But, hey, it's Tuesday and I'm sitting in the woods writing my book because I've finished all my deliverables for the month.

Trust the process.

Myth 3 - Freelancers will work for free

I'm really not sure where this one came from. Maybe it's the "free" in freelancer. But I prefer to label that as free for freedom.

Sure, some freelancers *do* work for free at times. There's a blurry line around when you should and shouldn't work for free.

The high-earning freelancer in me, who abides by growth principles of turning away low-paying clients and raising my prices regularly, wants to say you should *never* work for free.

But my personal growth and success have been contrary to this. In fact, in some cases, my best work has been work I've completed without a paying client.

Let's walk through when it's okay to work for free. Actually, let's start by making it clear when it's *not* okay to work for free.

When is it not okay to work for free?

The most common request for free work is "the test" or "the sample". There are differences between the two so it's important to establish these first.

A test is an assignment to prove your skills are what you sell them to be. This is a gamble on the employer/client's side just like making a new hire. You wouldn't hire a new barista without checking they could make coffee. So you likely won't hire a writer unless they can write.

Yes, there are circumstances where you hire trainees. And that's great. But, for this example, let's assume you're pitching yourself as a skilled freelancer.

When a prospective client proposes you complete a free test, they are de-risking themselves entirely. You could create a 2,500-word blog post that takes 5 days of your time, a ton of effort, exhausting resources, and stressing you out. And your end result? They go with someone else who submits a test blog post earlier.

My best advice for dealing with clients who ask for test assignments is to suggest they pay for your time.

Seriously.

Better clients will offer to pay for your time/service anyway. These are good clients. The ones who respect your time. The ones you want to win.

They're the opposite of the free test merchants, whose mantra *will* flow into your ongoing work with them. Clients who ask for free tests end up being those who are more than happy with scope creep, ask for edits of their own edits, then throw the whole project out, and expect your fee to cover their own confusion. More on scope creep when you've signed a customer later.

What you can say in these situations is: "I'd love to complete the test assignment and can complete it by XYZ. However, I would need compensating for my time at a rate of $$XYZ. This reflects my standard rate and will guarantee the work submitted will be of that caliber. I look forward to working on the project."

If they argue this further or get upset or offended, run away. These clients are rarely worth the effort. You could be spending this time winning real clients that make you happy.

It's hard to say no, at first. But when you redirect your energy into clients and work that make you productive, make you good money, and make you happy, you're on the path to freelance autonomy.

A good example of a hiring test process is that of Kyle Byers, director of organic search at Semrush. He shared his process of paid tests on his LinkedIn:

"My favorite way to evaluate and hire content writers, whether full-time or freelance:

(Two major steps, with two twists.)

First, always start with a paid trial assignment.

You can use content samples to filter out bad-fit candidates. But to choose who to hire in the end, you need paid trial assignments.

Why?

A writer's past work samples may have been:

- Heavily edited by someone else

- Turned in 3 months late

- Written based on an incredibly detailed outline/content brief

For the trial assignment, give the candidate clear expectations about what you want.

- Style

- Content goals and target audience/keyword

- Examples of what you're looking for

Best if you can provide a full content brief at this point, too.

Then, ask them to quote you their fee for the assignment.

Their quote will give you insight into how they think about their work and how much you can expect from them.

So, you shouldn't be looking for the cheapest quotes you can find here. In fact, it's a good idea to remind them before their quote that you're looking for quality--not quantity.

Twist number 1:

If their quote is too low, tell them why and let them revise it! (Assuming you're looking for a long-term partner who you can rely on for great work.)

Twist number 2:

After approving their quote, ask them to write only the first ~400-600 words of the article to start. Along with a basic outline of the remaining sections.

This way, you can give them feedback on their writing style and where the article is heading before they write the whole article.

If you have high standards, you'll find that 99% of writers can't nail it on the first try. And that's okay, as long as they're roughly in the right ballpark.

The more important thing is:

Can they take your feedback and quickly improve?

So, give them early feedback on their work, and watch how they apply your thinking to the rest of the article.

If it goes well, give them more feedback and a second paid trial assignment. By the end of the second assignment, you'll have a clear sense of how close they are to your standards and whether they're improving fast enough to work with.

Final tip:

In the long run, a "pretty good" writer who *wants* feedback (and is good at implementing it) is always better than a "really good" writer who gets offended or doesn't want to improve.

The process above is specifically designed to find folks who are already good AND care enough to get a lot better over time."

A sample, on the other hand, is a simpler matter. When a prospective client asks for a sample, you should already have one prepared.

If you're an experienced freelancer with relevant examples to the client you're pitching, *you've already got samples.*

I keep mine on my Medium site ready to cherry-pick or send the entire batch. See **www.bit.ly/exampleportfoliodk**

Pretty basic, right? That's for effort's sake. Your clients want to see samples of the work you're proposing to do for them. If you're a designer, they aren't judging you on your back-end SEO coding. If you're a writer, they want the quickest route to reading something you've written.

Links are just fine.

You can use any type of free site for this. There are portfolio-sharing sites designed specifically for this.

Here are a few to consider:

- Carrd
- Canva
- Notion
- read.cv
- Authory
- Clippings
- Contently
- Adobe Portfolio
- Journo Portfolio

You might want to include a portfolio on your own site if you have one. Web visitors who find you but don't know you can then see how great you are without needing to arrange a call or ask for a test assignment.

Do you see a common theme here? Every small change we make impacts the overall freelance experience. By simply collating your portfolio in one place, you don't need to go hunting for samples every time a client asks for one. By adding them to your website, you show potential clients that you're the real deal. The sales process becomes slicker. Trust is built immediately.

Keep your samples safe and public. You'll thank yourself in the future.

When is it okay to work for free?

I've completed free work in three scenarios (that I can recall):
1. Guest posts that will benefit me in the short or long term.
2. Favors for friends that might one day return the favor.
3. Community projects that make me feel good.

With guest posts, some freelance marketers might think this is something you only write for clients to help improve their SEO. But there are tons of benefits for guest posting when you're building an audience or raising your own profile.

I've included a guest post later in this book that I wrote for Superpath, a community for content marketers. I did this for free for several reasons:
1. I love the community and enjoy giving back.
2. I was going to repurpose it in this book so it was time well invested.
3. Writing such a post would increase my potential audience for products and services.

When you think of free work as genuine marketing, the "free" element becomes okay. As long as it's relevant to the niche, community, or industry you're in. This does mean, however, that you should be selective with free or guest posts. For example, writing a post to get a backlink to your site from an unknown site is almost worthless. But posting in a community that regularly looks for help with sourcing freelancers puts your name front and center.

I feel that "doing friends favors" needs some clarity. I don't endorse mates rates or free work just because someone is a friend. (Exception for small favors; but we're going to discuss mid to long-term projects.) At the end of the day, you are a business. And if you're doing work for free, you could be missing out on income or the opportunity to find income.

Doing friends favors does pay dividends when you stand a chance of receiving something back one day. That might be a referral, some business with them, or a case study.

One example I have is conducting an SEO audit for my friend Tom. We'd been online friends for a while after hanging around in the same industry. I did this for free when he asked for help for five reasons:

1. I like Tom very much; he's a really nice guy.
2. We have this unwritten agreement where we can DM each other almost anything and we'll help each other out.
3. One day, the company he works for might need my services and he has the confidence of referring someone he's tried and tested.
4. One day, he might go independent and need my services and he has the confidence of using someone he's tried and tested.

5. One day, he might get asked by a customer, friend, or colleague and he has the confidence of referring someone he's tried and tested.

All of these are true. Tom is really nice. We still help each other out almost every day. He did refer me to the company he was working for (resulting in over $80,000 worth of business). He did hire me when he went independent. He did refer me to another business in the same industry (resulting in $10,000 worth of work). I'd say that's making good of doing Tom a favor.

Oh, and he bought me a case of cider too. Told you he was nice!

Side note: you need to deliver here too. Just because you're doing a friend a favor doesn't mean you can drop your standards. Otherwise, it becomes a favor and nothing more.

I approach any work I do with that mindset. Be it a new customer, existing customer, customer who's given notice, a guest post on a publication that doesn't know me, or my personal site, recognizing that everything you post online (or offline if that's your line of work) is a potential business opportunity. How you present yourself and your work is part of what gets you hired.

This, really, is a story about the success of community. (More on niche and community later.) Without embedding myself into the industry I work in, I would only know Tom from afar. But our constant interactions, showing up in the same places, and having common interests made us obvious friends.

When you give to a community, you're one step closer to receiving something back.

And that doesn't have to be the niche you're in or the community you hang out in. It might be something close to your heart. For example, Maheen Kanwal, a freelance writer, says it's okay to work for free when "you're volunteering or for writing for an organization supporting a good cause. Be their voice. Give to the community."

Cici Asanga, another freelance writer, provided me with this nice list of when it's okay to work for free as a freelancer. I think #6 overrides them all.

1. When you are starting out
2. When you are taking a calculated risk
3. When you want a portfolio item
4. When you are struggling to get work and that might open doors
5. When you care about the cause (e.g. charities)
6. When you want to
7. To build goodwill

I replied to her comment with "I think #6 overrides them all! Only do free work when you want to!

I'm a big advocate of not working for free but there are circumstances where I do—and really quite a lot of them. But only because I WANT to."

"Working" also doesn't have to be exactly the services you offer either. This year, I'm volunteering at a game reserve in Africa *because I want to*. Endangered animals can't protect themselves from at-distance poachers and their natural habitats are being destroyed. Me writing a blog about this would have very little impact given my audience. But volunteering in the game reserve might.

Myth 4 - Freelancers don't pay tax

While it would be nice, freelancers do pay tax. However, becoming a "limited company" in the UK means you operate like a real business. It's not dodging tax or doing anything shady. You genuinely are a business. So, you must act like one.

If you hire an accountant, they look after all this for you. And I'm quite tempted to leave this section at that.

But for the sake of being helpful, I've drafted in my own accountant, Martin Brooks of Gold Stag Accounts, to author the next section...

It can be more tax efficient to become a Limited (Ltd) company in the UK, but you should always discuss the best setup with an accountant to see if it's the best route for you.

For tax saving reasons, it usually makes sense to go Ltd once your profits exceed £30,000. Other than the tax savings that can be made, you can also increase your cash flow as you don't have to make the large payments on account you would as operating as a sole trader.

Operating as a sole trader is still a great option for people looking to keep things simple and generally earning £30,000 or below, as there is only one tax return due each year.

Some freelancers feel they are too small or can't afford to hire an accountant and do their own taxes. In reality, self-assessment tax returns usually cost under £200, and accountants can often save hun-

dreds or sometimes thousands with tax savings and planning, which pays for itself.

It's also worth noting that the timing is important if you're looking to mortgage or remortgage as most lenders will want to see two years' books in either sole trader or Ltd company format, and more and more lenders are requesting accountant verification of earnings these days.

My top three tips for any freelancer operating as a sole trader or Ltd company are:

- Open a business bank account - the good ones are all free
- Use cloud accounting software
- Work with an accountant

Being organized is key to staying on top of your own finances and following the steps above will put you in good stead.

Tax saving tips for Ltd companies:

- Trivial benefits up to £300 per tax year as long as each transaction doesn't exceed £50
- Company pension contributions (reduces profit and corporation tax)
- Use of home allowance (claim actual percentages of your household costs rather than a simple flat rate)

Sole traders can also claim a decent amount of working-from-home expenses, so it's definitely worth taking the time to calculate this and include it in your accounts.

Since using Martin as my accountant, he's opened my eyes to the things I can legitimately claim expenses on. And by simply having a business bank account and cloud accounting software, I'm more aware of claiming for everything I'm entitled to; which in the long term saves me thousands per year.

When you start to earn good money and have "spare" money, this is crucial to building a buffer for the times when you might not have any work. We'll introduce how and when to set money aside later in the book.

Now that we've dispelled some of the most common freelancing myths, it's time to set yourself up for autonomy (without feeling guilty that you're being productive and successful).

CHAPTER 3

SETTING YOURSELF UP FOR FREELANCE AUTONOMY

In a traditional book on becoming a freelancer, this chapter would be about owning the right equipment, having enough money saved to get you through a period of time where you might not get any work, or where to look online for your first gigs.

This chapter is about setting yourself up to be surrounded by people and resources that will help and inspire your freelance career.

This chapter is about setting the tone to empower yourself to achieve autonomy.

This chapter is about overcoming self-objections and fear that being autonomous is synonymous with greedy, lazy, or arrogant.

Let's start there.

When autonomy gets confused with arrogance

The fear of appearing anything other than compliant is something freelancers often fight themselves over. Especially those used to having a (bad) manager in a full-time role.

Moving from working for someone else to working for yourself is *hard*. You quite literally switch positions and become the business owner. You're also the CMO, head of sales, operations manager, and general dogs body.

You have to put *your business* first.

But what does that mean?

It means several things. Some of which might be changes to how you work and communicate. Some of these might feel drastic.

That's okay. Whenever we (humans) make a change, it feels wrong and we are resistant. I use the word "we" because it's how the brain works. Everybody does it; even if it's subconsciously. Part of the brain—the amygdala—interprets change as a threat and releases the hormones for fear, fight, or flight. Acceptance doesn't come into it. Until you train it to.

Now, training your brain is hard. Bloody hard. In The Chimp Paradox—a book on mind management by Professor Steve Peters, we're introduced to our inner chimp. That's the part of you that swears at drivers who cut you up on the road and lashes out when someone offends you. It's your natural instinct until you train it not to be. And the only way to do that is with conscious mind management. Over time, you'll learn that there is no consequence to *not* swearing at that driver. They will drive off either way. You will drive off either way. So, you stop yourself, accept their poor driving, and get on with your day.

We can apply this principle to setting yourself up for freelance autonomy. But the idea of telling our clients we no longer accept sales calls or want to work *our* productive hours feels like we are above them when you first try to move to this model. And when you communicate it wrong, it comes off that way to your prospect or client too.

The simple process of explaining how you work, and how it benefits your clients, removes any perceived arrogance, laziness, or any of the other negative misconceptions that people associate with you doing your utmost to be productive.

Sounds tough? It's not. I promise. All you need to do is to spend half an hour writing a template then tweak it every time a risky client asks for a call or meeting to discuss your services.

Note: While I'm pro asynchronous communications, there may still be a time for a real-time meeting. Use your judgment here rather than flat-out refusing to speak to anyone ever again.

Even if you become a meeting no-er like me, it doesn't mean everyone else will see this as a good thing.

Tamara Jensen, a project manager at T-Mobile, spoke at a Slack-related session about how to cancel more meetings. She's leading efforts at her company to replace unnecessary meetings with Slack, though adoption has been uneven across various teams.

"No matter what Slack does, some people are just going to have meeting FOMO. That takes a little bit of training. People have to get comfortable saying no and trust that it's going to be offline and available to them."

Here's an example of an exchange that came in literally as I was typing the paragraphs above. I'll share everything word for word:

"Exciting content marketing opportunity!

Hi Dominic, I hope you're well!

I'm currently working for a hyper-growth global unified communications company specializing in mediation between voice and IT Infrastructure.

To support with their progressive product roadmap and continuous high growth, they're seeking an experienced content marketer with a passion for content, web, and social, to support in the delivery of their ambitious, varied, and fast-paced content strategy.

I felt as though your profile strongly aligned with what my client is looking for, and I'd love to discuss this opportunity with you further!

Do you have any time tomorrow for a call?"

I could down tools and jump at this "Exciting content marketing opportunity" at short notice and without any context. But, instead, I'm going to send a short reply with the goal of obtaining the information I need to decide whether or not they are a good fit for me.

"Hey, I have time later this week but would like to learn more about the opportunity first. Which company is it and are they looking for full time or freelance?"

It is a permanent role, please find the JD attached and let me know if you would still be interested in discussing further!

Very quickly, I can filter that one out as not a good fit. I'm not looking for a permanent role so I decline. 30 minutes saved. What you could do here is offer your freelance services as an alternative. While most companies are set in their ways by the time you see a job description, some are open to filling the gap or hiring a superior alternative for a period of time.

Araminta Robertson, a former freelance writer, received this response when doing just that:

*"I have received positive feedback from ** about your application. As this is a part-time engagement, we can offer you a freelance contract to begin with, this can be extended into a full time contract at a later date. The contract rate we can offer is $**** per month, and you are expected to work 24 hours per week."*

So, it does work!

In reality, I have so few customers that I communicate synchronously with that it's a novelty when I do.

Try this out for a template:

"Hi there, thanks for reaching out about my services. I'm thrilled you think we can work together. Before I engage in any calls, I like to ensure we're both aligned so we don't take up each other's time unnecessarily. Here's my services list with associated pricing. Once you're okay with these, let's work out how we take the next steps."

This is a tame version but it helps you filter out clients who can't afford you and time wasters who don't know what they need and are looking for free advice.

Note: as discussed in the previous section, there is a time and place for free work. Use your judgment here too. A free 15-minute consultancy call *could* land you a $10,000 project.

The stronger version of this template helps set the tone for future asynchronous communications. Here's a basic response that Rodolphe Dutel, founder of Remotive, a job board and community for remote workers, uses every time someone asks him for a call:

"I get tons of call requests on Twitter, LinkedIn or by email:

- Would you be available for a 15 min talk about it? Thanks!
- Can we have a call in the coming days to discuss opportunities?
- How about a quick meeting/call next week?

Most requests are first contacts and are generic or lack context.

People schedule intro calls because that's what (traditional) business etiquette suggests.

A 30-minute intro call means 15 minutes of introducing each other, then 15 minutes of exchanging context.

Most of those conversations would be better asynchronous.

I've been using this canned response:

Hi XYZ, it's great to meet you - how can I help you? We're transitioning to being an asynchronous company, meaning we try to only communicate via email, voicemail, and video (e.g. Loom).

Excited to hear from you/read you on [insert email address] - many thanks!"

Rodolphe also shares his findings from using this template for 12 months:

- Nearly everyone has a positive response.
- 75% email me back; 25% don't.
- Few continue pushing for a call.
- People who can't email what they need are likely to be high maintenance.

More often than not, both Rodolphe's and my clients are absolutely fine with this. To some, it will be completely alien. Even the thought of recording a video might scare off a client in some industries. And they might not even have a camera. Again, use your judgment here; but do make a conscious effort to reduce meetings that don't turn into revenue or you at least gain something useful from them.

As a clear example of making this successful, in the past week, I've had zero real-time meetings. Instead, I communicate with two clients on Slack, one on Microsoft Teams, and one via email. I check my messages in my own time and share documents and ideas as and when I need to. And this works. But only because I made it clear this is how and why I work this way.

Since becoming a freelancer, and since adopting asynchronous communications, my productivity has increased at least 300%.

I say "at least" because that's all I can measure. Projects that took three days in a full-time role take one day. Tasks that took three hours are completed in an hour. But I also have many other things to do that I didn't when I was in a full-time role. However, as mentioned above, accounting, marketing, and communications can be streamlined by simply changing your mindset and using the right tools.

The same is true for the tools you find productive and working the hours you feel productive. To achieve autonomy, it must be about the way you work.

For example, I have a lot of clients who are Microsoft partners. Naturally, they want to use Microsoft's products like Word and PowerPoint. But I am so much more productive when using Google Docs or Google Slides. So, when I'm working solo on something (like a blog post that I will upload or a presentation that I will present—anything that doesn't need multi-party collaboration), I explain that I'll be more efficient in delivering what they've asked for using my tool of choice. There's no downside for them as they only need to read the blog post and approve it. Or it's a presentation they will watch as I present. It just doesn't make sense to use tools that lessen my productivity if I'm the only one using them. This is true to the extent that you don't even need to tell people what they're watching. Save yourself a task.

In some (larger) businesses, there may be security risks associated with using new software. Respect this and don't expect a client paying you $5,000 a month to change their task management system to Trello just because you like it. Sometimes there does need to be compromise.

When you can use what enables you to achieve more in a smaller time period or use what helps you feel more productive, do so.

At the core, it's all about communication. If you don't ask, you don't get.

We've touched on imposter syndrome in the previous chapter but there's no harm in reviewing how you should communicate with your clients.

Let's flesh this out a little more.

How should you communicate with your clients?

As a freelancer, there are several stakeholders you may find yourself communicating with:

- Direct manager/client
- Your client/direct manager's manager
- Director/C-level
- Accounts
- Subject matter experts
- Peer-level collaborators

Each of these may need different forms of communication. Within those forms of communication, there will likely be nuances as every person is different regardless of their job title.

Types of communication include:

- Real-time one-to-one calls
- Real-time group calls
- Face-to-face meetings
- Email
- Asynchronous messaging (Like Slack, Microsoft Teams, etc.)
- Asynchronous video (like Loom, Tella, etc.)
- Reports
- Contracts

- Interviews
- Invoices

Frequency of communication includes:
- Instant
- Hourly
- Ad-hoc (as and when; the preferred option for autonomous freelancers)
- Daily
- Weekly
- Twice weekly
- Every other week
- Monthly
- Quarterly
- Yearly
- Never

Now, let's match our stakeholders to the types and frequencies of communication. In the old-fashioned business world, where people have meetings for the sake of it, this would lean towards overcommunicating, keeping everyone in the loop all the time, and being "always available."

This matrix might look a little scary at first. You might wonder how on Earth some of the "nevers" can be possible and if they are healthy for a working relationship. Believe me, I've seen every objection under the sun. If you want to achieve genuine autonomy as a freelancer, increasing the effectiveness of your asynchronous communications and decreasing your dependency on synchronous communications are huge steps in the right direction.

Note: this matrix is a guide and you don't need to treat it as gospel. Some projects *do* need real-time collaboration and that's fine. Also, the key theme of autonomy is working on your own terms. So if your craft and productivity are genuinely improved by real-time calls, go for it.

But don't make them default by habit. Of course, if you're working in an office space with your clients, face-to-face is likely easier. But in very few freelance vocations are face-to-face meetings *needed* for communications. Even if you paint film sets, the work you do on set is different from the communications that get you there.

If you're still reluctant to give up on meeting for meeting's sake, here's one last effort from me:

Of 182 people surveyed by the University of North Carolina, 65% said meetings keep them from completing their work, 71% said meetings are unproductive and inefficient, and 64% said meetings come at the expense of deep thinking.

	Real-time 1:1	Real-time group	Face-to-face	Email	Async comms	Reports
Client	Ad-hoc	Ad-hoc	Networking	Contracts	Ad-hoc	Monthly
Client's boss	Never	Never	Networking	Contracts	Ad-hoc	Monthly
Directors	Never	Never	Never	Contracts	Never	Monthly
Accounts	Never	Never	Never	Invoices	Never	Never
SMEs	Interviews	Interviews	Networking	Never	Ad-hoc	Monthly
Peer level	Never	Interviews	Networking	Never	Ad-hoc	Monthly

Some of the "ad-hocs" in this table might be all day every day. But they could also be once a week or once a month. Use whatever works best in that situation to provide the most effective outcome.

In the rows for the client's boss and directors, this may also be different if your work is for that level. In this case, the matrix is not applicable. But, for the vast majority of freelance craft, "client" is sufficient for establishing when and how to communicate with your clients.

Notice there is no *instant* messaging. Replacing instant messaging with asynchronous messaging removes the always-on mentality that more often than not leads to burnout. Sure, you might reply instantly. But set the expectations that your messenger app is asynchronous.

In reality, the only people who need to be "always-available" are emergency responders and security personnel. And even they take it in shifts.

This is why email need not be used except for formal documents that need a paper trail. The asynchronous element is covered by a tool like Slack or Microsoft Teams. There may be exceptions when you or your client doesn't pay for Slack. As of January 2023, the free plan only saves the last 10,000 messages on your workspace. Think about that when you share information and need to save documents, ideas, or conversations.

"Email" includes online apps like DocuSign so there's less faff uploading and signing documents. By reducing the number of tools, number of clicks, and dependency on real-time and legacy tools, we move a step closer to autonomy.

Again, just to stress, if *your* most productive method is different to this, stick with it. But don't do so because you're scared of not speaking to your customer on a daily basis.

It's likely this matrix is nothing like how you currently work. And that's okay (for now). Later in this section, we'll cover how to introduce asynchronous communications with new customers. Forcing or requesting habits with current customers is an entirely different challenge. And it may take considerable time.

Think about the aspects of your templated response for new clients (that we'll make in a few paragraphs time) that are most important and drip feed them to customers who you think take up too much time without providing value in return. A suggestion for improved productivity or faster ROI will go down better than a note saying you're never going to phone or email them again.

Before you start to communicate with each type of stakeholder in a set way, it's important to set expectations and parameters.

For example, you may liaise with your client on a one-to-one level via Slack or email every day. And that's okay until you sign another customer and can't dedicate time to fielding queries when you should be writing code or designing a graphic for someone else. Likewise, it pays to be prepared for the rare scenario when the owner of the business drops you a meeting request out of the blue.

In your contract, make sure you protect yourself from undercommunication and make it clear how it is both acceptable and productive to communicate. Again, explain to your customers *why* you work this way and the benefits for *them*.

Doing this *before* you sign a contract and start working with them is crucial. Otherwise, you end up in territory no freelancer wants to find themselves in: unbillable work.

I once thought I had a slam dunk and skipped the key process of defining how we'd communicate.

What I should have done was:

- Agree to create all documents as Word documents (they were a Microsoft partner)
- Save them all on the client's SharePoint site
- Accept revisions as comments on said docs

Because I skipped this step, we had numerous calls where I had to teach them how to use Google Docs, I had to recreate my Google Sheet tracker as a SharePoint site, and I had to present the free admin I'd done to make sure we were finally aligned.

You might think this is part and parcel of dealing with customers. But it doesn't need to be unbilled. Either plan time for this or be clear with your communication plan (including written communications and documentation) from day one.

If you've included your processes, how you work, and what makes you productive in your personal branding, none of this will be a surprise to your new client. They sign the contract and you start a prosperous relationship.

What if there's pushback?

You have three options here. It's a bit like poker.

1. Fold: say yes to this customer now (and forever); setting the tone for future engagements.
2. Check: stand firm and just say no. (This does work sometimes.)

3. Raise: (the stakes). Explain why your prices/processes/communications preferences are beneficial. Sound familiar? Do this upfront to save time during the crucial contracting phase.

Seriously, write a template for this. Even better—let's write one together now.

Thanks for your email. - always thank the sender.

I understand your concern about working asynchronously. - show empathy with the reason they countered your proposal.

Some of my previous clients expressed the same feelings when we first started working together. - make them feel they're not alone and being awkward.

Here we've been friendly and reassured our client that we understand their ask. But what we must now do is prove your way works. If you have other clients who let you work in your preferred (autonomous) way, note them here. We're taking the same approach as we would create a landing page.

Unbounce, the landing page builder tool, has an excellent "anatomy of a landing page" infographic that shares all the crucial parts that turn landing pages into money magnets. Here are the ones we're borrowing:

1. Headline
2. Supporting copy
3. Social proof
4. Reinforcing statement
5. Benefits

6. Call to action

If you don't have customers you're able to name-drop here, that's okay too. You can use your own business as an example. Explain the before and after of working in your most productive state. If you can, include figures to reinforce your opinion. If you can say you've taken your blog writing process from 8 hours to 6 hours, that's a 25% increase in productivity. If you show your graphic designs have visually improved since changing your work style, there's no stronger case. If you can show how you've made more money since you made the change, your prospect just became your client. After all, they're hiring you to make them money.

After our social proof (case study/namedrop/testimonial), we must reinforce the point we're making.

It's down to my work style that XYZ is able to continuously achieve these staggering results.

After this reminder, remind your customer of the benefits (that you should have already in your email thread).

Since revising my process, customers have seen faster turnaround times, fewer revisions on their part, and a higher ROI on services we've contracted.

These are example benefits you can tailor. What's important here is that the benefits translate to making your client's life easier. That's why people hire freelancers. You have a skill they need and can't complete in-house.

Here's a reminder of the contract [link] for you to sign.

The most important part of this email is the end (contrary to what email marketers say about the subject heading). You're already engaged to the point where you've sent a contract. Your client is reading your email in the hope that you say yes to whatever they've requested (which you have changed their mind on). The final point of the email is where they were originally expecting a "yes". But you've done such a good job of selling the way you work that the next step is for *them* to say yes.

Remember, for new clients, drip feed these details to suggest positive changes that will make your client's life easier (and yours more productive).

You've just taken a huge step towards autonomy.

Here's the response for you to copy and paste/ type up yourself:

Thanks for your email.

I understand your concern about working asynchronously.

Some of my previous clients expressed the same feelings when we first started working together.

It's down to my work style that XYZ is able to continuously achieve these staggering results.

Since revising my process, customers have seen faster turnaround times, fewer revisions on their part, and a higher ROI on services we've contracted.

Here's a reminder of the contact [link] for you to sign.

Don't forget to mention the actual staggering results, testimonials, and links. Simply copying this text won't nab you a client who wants to work asynchronously.

What to do when your contact leaves the company

A huge part of making your communications with clients autonomous is forming an understanding with your main point of contact. You should, after time, bounce off each other because you work so well together. After all, every freelance relationship is two-way.

But what do you do when that contact, who you know so well and you know they will fight your corner, leaves the business?

There are two scenarios you could find yourself in:
1. Your contact plans to leave and does a handover.
2. Your contact leaves all of a sudden and you don't know who to speak with.

In the former, work with your contact to meet their replacement and help plan your next batch of work. If you have a purchase order or contract in place, it's simply a new contact. If you don't, or your retainer is up for renewal, you may have to sell your services again. Achieve this by compiling all the work you've completed and planned with your previous contact. Showcasing how important you are to the company goes a long way. And in most cases, your new contact will want to hit the ground running so carrying on as normal is beneficial to them.

In the second case, like if a company announces sudden layoffs, you may not have the opportunity to meet a new contact or help compile a handover. In extreme cases, you may not even get a new contact as everyone you know disappears overnight.

Sounds extreme? It is. But trust me. It happened and I had no idea what was going to happen to my future work with this client.

Here's what I did to ensure I kept the work I had penciled in for the next six months. For reference, the client had signed a purchase order for 17 blog posts over the course of the year and I'd only delivered 3 at this point. This enterprise client pays on delivery at the end of every month.

After announcing they'd been laid off on LinkedIn (this is still the only communication I've had to date), I first messaged my contact to say how sorry I was to hear this. I did this because 1) I was sad they'd lost their job and 2) I had a good working relationship with them and would like to work with them wherever they end up next.

I didn't expect them to want to help me. They now have a new job to look for. More so, they no longer work for the company so have no access to help me out. At this stage, I realized how important it was to move quickly.

My next port of call was to go up the chain. I happened to know who my contact's direct manager was so I emailed them. But I got no response over the next two days. Guess what? They'd been laid off too. I only discovered this formally after looking back through an old blog post draft we'd worked on together. Their Google account has been deleted so their old comments read **"Deleted user commented: XYZ."**

Not knowing who was next up the chain in terms of seniority, I emailed my billing contact to see if they could push me in the right direction. Allowing them a night to respond, I was sent to someone in a similar role who eventually pushed me in the direction of my soon-to-be contact.

When I finally made it to who is my new contact for submitting blog posts, I took my time to explain what I'd already done in terms of deliverables, what I had planned, and the agreement between me and the company.

By taking the initiative and laying out what I had to deliver, I held the advantage. I was in control. Very quickly, my outstanding posts were published and we agreed on my next set of deliverables. Over the course of a week, I'd gone from worrying about losing $33,000 worth of work to business as usual.

Of course, in some cases, this may not happen. Layoffs internally could mean winding down external contractors too. But the sooner you act, the sooner you'll know where you stand.

This section didn't have anything to do with autonomy. But autonomy without customers makes for a useless freelancer.

Forming habits to achieve autonomy

"Most people don't have that willingness to break bad habits. They have a lot of excuses, and they talk like victims."

These are the words of Carlos Santana, thought of as one of the best guitarists in history.

Breaking bad habits and forming new habits takes work. And if you don't buy into this now, you should put this book down and think about whether you want to achieve freelance autonomy or are happy with your current setup.

Unless you're a friend who bought this book to support me, I'd wager you do already realize you can be more productive and change your work-life balance. So, for those sticking with it, here's what you must do to empower *yourself*.

Turning a new thing into a habit apparently takes 66 days. So there really is no time like the present.

While writing this book, I started learning Portuguese. By day 12, I could recall common phrases, name loads of food, and tell you that an armadillo reads the newspaper (seriously).

However, to learn a full language using Duolingo, Brianne Huntsman—a freelance blogger—found you will need to spend a minimum of 130 minutes per day for a full 180 days. That's commitment. Commitment to forming a new habit.

If you're unfamiliar with the concept of habits, it's not just cracking your knuckles (guilty) or picking your nose. Habits are "small decisions you make and actions you perform every day."

That's the definition from James Clear, who authors Atomic Habits, which has sold over 3 million copies.

I read this in 2019 and it did not change my life.

What it did do was reinforce all the good habits I'd picked up in my full-time employed career and confirmed I was ready to go it alone as a freelancer.

How to use habits to empower autonomy

Habits are the things you do without thinking. When something becomes a habit, it is literally your body working autonomously. You do it without realizing and it becomes a natural part of your day.

There are both good and bad habits freelancers develop.

The bad ones restrict autonomy and become a drain on productivity. These are things like saying yes to meetings without knowing what you're walking into, overworking to meet imaginary deadlines, and taking on work with little value (monetary or otherwise).

The good ones empower autonomy. They change how you go about your working day. They happen on autopilot without you taking time out of your day to decide whether you do them.

Examples of these range from tiny things like turning on your laptop to power up every morning as you get into the shower (separate tasks!) to understanding when you've hit a stale patch during deep work and being comfortable to go do something else.

If your office space is en route to the bathroom, why not turn your laptop on? You might only save a minute as you no longer have to wait for everything to boot up, but if you work 260 days per year, that's over 4 hours saved. That's a half day off.

In the middle of the scale, I'm going to reference the 5S methodology introduced in the Lean Six Sigma principles. In short, this means keeping a tidy workplace to declutter your mind. Your workplace reflects your work.

Lucy Rose wrote in a guest blog for Carl Pullein, "A Princeton University study found clutter makes it harder for people to focus on particular tasks. Specifically, the researchers discovered that the visual cortex is easily overwhelmed by task-irrelevant objects, making it difficult to allocate attention and complete set tasks efficiently. A clean and clear workspace eliminates distractions and can therefore help employees better concentrate on the task at hand."

The 5S' are:

Sort | Set in order | Shine | Standardize | Sustain

By **sorting** your workspace into an environment without clutter, you minimize the chance of distraction. This doesn't mean you have to remove everything. Personal touches are associated with comfort rather than productivity; however, nobody is productive in an uncomfortable environment. But it does mean removing unnecessary paperwork, unused devices, and general clutter. My regular workstation includes a stand-up desk, laptop, podcast mic, lamp for video recording, and a corkboard on my wall. That's it.

When you've sorted what you do and don't need, **setting them in order** means making them accessible when you need them. In a traditional office setting, this means moving the printer to the department that uses it the most and displaying sales stats in the sales office rather than the team having to get up to check the figures. In your workspace, use this to store your most-used devices nearby, keep the books you reference most at the top of the pile, and hide anything you use less than once a week. Make putting everything back in the right place a habit and cheat your way to optimizing your workspace.

Shine includes the act of keeping everything clean. For obvious reasons like bacteria and dust, yes. But it also includes the psychology behind working in a clean environment. Tidy desk; tidy mind.

Standardize is most appropriate in large organizations but you can apply it in the freelancer or remote worker role too. By creating standard processes (with regards to your workplace), you stand more of a chance of making what you've worked on a habit. If your standard process is to return your reference book to your shelf when you're done with it (as opposed to leaving it on your desk for the rest of the day), then you will stick to it. If your standard process is to leave it on the desk, you will fall into the trap of thinking it's okay. Untidy desk; untidy mind.

Sustain is the hardest of the 5S' to achieve. But, by standardizing, you help yourself form good habits that make sustaining your new working environment all that easier. Unless your workspace is really, really bad, this is a lot less effort than it sounds. Just remember that it's another cog you're turning that helps you in the long run.

At the more extreme end of the scale, we see things like understanding our minds and bodies. For example, I know when I have hit the lower half of how productive I can be so I do something about it. For a while, I thought this meant starting another task. But context switching and trying to cram everything in during "working hours" often meant I just performed that task less well than when I was fully focused.

Instead, I now acknowledge that I'm not performing as well as I can and go for a dog walk. Or I drive to the coffee shop in town. Or I read a book. Or I might even turn on the PlayStation for an hour.

Cynics will say that's time wasted.

But taking however long feels right to recharge quite literally recharges you. I can normally work for a burst of 3 hours in the morning. Then I walk my dogs for about an hour, check my social media, emails, Slack, then have lunch. My next burst of uninterrupted work is usually shorter, but I achieve more and at a higher quality because I am energized.

The alternative is staring at a screen with writer's block or creating dispassionate content. If I persisted with either of these, I'd likely have to do them again anyway.

There are so many small habits you can change that allow you to work when and how you want.

Habits worth changing if you're serious about autonomy

- Removing reliance on synchronous communication
- Work on your personal brand in your downtime
- Create templates for repetitive processes or tasks
- Productize your services where possible
- Create canned responses to objections
- Tidy your workspace on a regular basis
- Take breaks when you get stuck
- Work when you're productive
- Say no to time sucks

Here are some more habits I crowdsourced from Twitter:

> "Use comfy spaces to read so my brain feels dopamine and retains information better."
>
> Helen Duffy, B2B SaaS marketing consultant.

> "Knowing when to mix it up if things aren't working. Pause and do something else or get out for a change of scene."
>
> Martin Dewar, freelance content and social media marketer.

> "As soon as a problem comes up with a client, I immediately add language about it into my contract (for future projects). Over time, this results in a contract that does a really good job of protecting me."
>
> Jessie Wood, content strategist.

> "Knowing your niche and who your ideal client/project is and being very clear and up-front about it."
>
> Angie Moody, CEO & co-founder of Ruby Money.

Sounds like hard work? It's not really. You do most of these once and you've saved yourself from ever doing them again.

Take templates or canned responses. The next time you find yourself writing a response to an objection from a client, save it. The next time you need to create a PowerPoint deck with a content marketing strategy, save it.

Older generations (generalizing much) take pride in taking forever to put together work that could be completed quicker. And do I dare mention the word, shortcut?

> **"Short cuts make long delays."**
> **J.R.R. Tolkien, The Fellowship of the Ring**

Tolkien had a point. And he made it very well by creating rather long journeys in rather long books. Every time they tried a shortcut, several chapters appeared. But, with some context and preparation, you can create "shortcuts" that help put some of your work on autopilot.

When I worked as a business consultant, templates were the name of the game. Not only did everything look on-brand but it saved so much time. Why opt to create a new version of the same thing every time when you can save the first one as a template and reuse it each time?

Note: do actually save a template copy. Then save a new copy every time you use the template. Otherwise, yes, Tolkien has absolutely got you there.

You can apply this to almost anything you create a deck for, any sales materials like proposals and contracts, and documents you add your logo or contact details on. If you make more than one of something in your early days as a freelancer, your future self will thank you a dozen times.

All is well and good *talking* about habits. Forming them and forgetting them. But without the right inspiration and the right people backing you, it's hard to execute on your proposals.

The biggest habit you can change or double down on—if you're serious about autonomy—is to surround yourself with positive influences.

Surround yourself with positive influences

Positive influences are those who make your day better. They inspire you to be like them, they push you to be better, they help you become the best version of you. They share real stories and aren't afraid to fail. They succeed and share their learnings along the way. They build communities rather than followers. And they have their community's best interests at heart.

Positive influences aren't those who have loads of followers, constantly promote their products, or push that their way is the only way. They aren't those with the high-price products and loads of people downloading their courses. They aren't those who shout the loudest or have the biggest budgets.

"Surrounding yourself" means in-person, online, in your working environment, and even in your mailbox.

If you work at a customer's site, there may be toxic personalities or clashes in work styles. Online, you may feel pressured to follow certain influencers because everyone else is. In your working environment, that could be your partner who doesn't appreciate how you work. And your mailbox is often the worst place to find negative influences. Everyone wants your attention and you feel a sense of dread if you don't read each one.

Here's how to turn these negative influences into positive ones.

If your negative influences are literally surrounding you, remove yourself from the environment. I did this when I was working full-time for a company full of loud and unproductive people. The most important part of their day was making sure the lunch order was right, then popping out for another cigarette and announcing it was time for the coffee run. When they were actually working, it mostly involved some form of shouting. So, I left. The office, that is.

One day, I just stopped coming into the office. This wasn't quite as drastic as it sounds because I sometimes worked from home or went to visit customers. But I thought everybody would appreciate my output if it was more efficient and of better quality. So, I did something about it.

As freelancers, we mostly operate solo and in our own homes. But, if you don't, you can still empower yourself to be productive. My advice of "just leave" might be caveated by chatting with your client about this first. If your work relies on working with them *physically* then there is an obvious red flag here too. However, I know a lot of contractors in large organizations that have done this and nobody has batted an eyelid. It's about judging the situation and making an executive decision after weighing up the pros and cons.

Will anybody mind? If yes, explain the benefits. If no, it's probably all in your head anyway.

Since the coronavirus pandemic, businesses have been facing a tough time trying to get staff (permanent and freelance) "back to the office". If ever there was an eye-opener to office unproductivity and giving people a choice of working environment, it was the big unplanned and unmeasured experiment of 2020-2021.

In an article for Slate, Alison Green collected snippets of why people *aren't* going back to the office—even when some companies made it mandatory. I share the best responses here:

"I have to go in one day a week, but I don't want to do more than that. It is a really nice building, with plenty of meeting space, cafeteria with good food, coffee shop, gym, etc. As nice as that is, I still prefer yoga pants and my cat as my only co-worker. I get my own bathroom, full kitchen, and no commute. They really can't beat that."

That's comfort.

"I feel like single offices (we have an open plan), child/pet/elder care stipends, or honestly a factual, mathematical explanation of why on-site work is beneficial would go further toward getting people in."

That's accessibility.

"The C-suite at my company has been trying to bring everyone back to the office three days a week for about a year now, and my department (IT) has just collectively gone, 'Nah.' ... Literally we just didn't do it. Some people did at first, but when they saw no one else was showing up, they mostly stopped too."

That's empowered autonomy.

"My office is bringing everyone back for no reason and it is not working. We are 'required' to be in the office three days a week but no one is doing it except for a handful of people who like working in the office."

That's personal preference.

"My company actually did try pushing the issue, but honestly it just backfired. HR sent out angry emails about how we needed to be in the office, a few people went in, those people saw that the office was still empty so they stopped coming in, repeat a few times, and now we all know that blatantly ignoring the higher-ups won't necessarily get us fired lol. They would've been better off just letting it go sooner."

That's just a bad HR team.

"My company had mandated three days a week back in the office, but I moved an eight-hour drive away, so I just said I couldn't. This is a combination of me being at a point in my career where I have the confidence and capital to say no and knowing that there is other work out there for someone with my experience level. I could easily find a job, even if the job market was slow. The pandemic has just made it so most of the jobs I see posted in my field are remote, which gives me even more confidence."

That's autonomy.

"What would get me back is real flexibility. I'm happy to work a hybrid schedule, but I have no interest in working a job where the number of days I come to the office per week or per month are kept track of. If I have a month where it makes sense for me to spend most of my time in the office, that's fine. If I have a month where it's just not necessary and I don't feel like putting on real pants, I would hope that my employer could be as flexible with me as I'm willing to be with them. If I am doing my job to the expected standard, I hope that my employer can work with me in truly being flexible and not just worry about Butts in Seats."

That's flexibility.

"To me, the biggest thing is being able to clearly explain why it's necessary. Don't give some vague explanation like 'it's time' or 'we think it's better' but have a specific reason why you think it's better to convince your employees that it's beneficial. And that reason needs to be one that will hold up once people get there. Nothing is going to kill people's enthusiasm about returning to the office quicker than showing up and realizing that it's exactly the same as working from home—also known as 'you made me commute 45 minutes for this? Why??'"

That's sensibility.

Overall, there's an overwhelming consensus that the in-person, in-office, impossible-to-work environment is not favorable.

That's why I just left (the office).

Of course, if your in-person trips are productive, enjoyable, and surrounded by positive influences, keep it up. But don't mandate set days and times. Discuss on an ad-hoc basis when it's beneficial for you or anyone to attend. That might be every day. It might be once a year.

If you work *at home*, you might be sharing a workspace with your partner or housemate. Even if you get on great with them outside of work, they may not share the same beliefs about what you do or how you do it.

My girlfriend works 8-5 Monday to Thursday and barely steps away from her desk. If I had to do that, I'd have quit a long time ago. I'm genuinely flabbergasted at how in tune with her laptop she is for the entire day. Sometimes I start a conversation and she doesn't hear it because she's so engrossed with her work. That might work for her (though she's never tried anything else) but it sounds like hell to me.

If that does *genuinely* work for you, I say crack on. But be honest with yourself when evaluating. I'd argue you're not reading this book if you love being governed by the clock.

I mention this because when I finish by 9am and rush off to walk the dogs, work on a personal project, or just have the rest of the day off, I appreciate how she must feel. I earn more than her and, most of the time, work less. This is manageable by the right personality; and we are both blessed with similar mindsets on income and ways of working. As long as we're happy, healthy, and earning enough money to remain happy and healthy, who are we to question how we work?

But I have heard horror stories, which increased during the coronavirus pandemic, about couples splitting up, housemates moving out, and even neighbors falling out. Remember the section on the 5S? If you need a clean working environment and your housemate is a slob, there's going to be a problem sustaining that.

This might seem trivial if you don't have this problem. But setting boundaries and expectations goes a long way when you're operating your own freelance business in a shared workspace with someone who doesn't appreciate how you work. I'm not suggesting moving out (though it could be the best course of action in extreme circumstances), but a frank conversation is a must.

On Twitter, don't follow people that make you feel less important, small, or like you're failing. Even if they have 100,000 followers and all your friends and peers follow them, *you* are in control of your feed.

Instead, follow people that share relevant topics, provide helpful insights, and care about their followers. The same applies to LinkedIn, Facebook, Instagram, or anywhere you hang out online.

And it definitely applies in your mailbox.

It's 2023 (it was when I was writing this anyway) and a huge amount of people and businesses still rely on, and are reluctant to move away from, email.

Some have good reasons. Most don't. But, because of this, your mailbox is likely a dumping ground for unwanted messages, task procrastination, and unbilled time. On top of that, people are trying to sell you things, con you into FOMO, and steal all your money if you click the wrong link.

To combat these negative influences, apply these three habits (remember those?):

1. Unsubscribe to everything you don't want or need.
2. Check notifications where they belong.
3. Set up gated.com

Unsubscribing is obvious. When you're on a list, remove yourself from it. While your current habit might be to just delete the email, all you're doing is a temporary fix. Instead, move your cursor a little more and hit unsubscribe. At first, this takes some time to cleanse your inbox. But, I get about 10 emails a week. One I subscribe to. Then a handful from customers and some order confirmations.

This is achieved by unsubscribing but also by turning off notifications by email. If you use apps like Microsoft Teams, you get notifications in-app. The same for Trello and Slack and pretty much every app that sends you a notification. Simply turning off the email notifications will, however, lend itself to missing notifications. You must change your habit.

I wrote a post about "notification fatigue" and, while I was assembling it, realized that it's completely our fault. Yes, technology provides the things that drain productivity. But we say yes to them by default. Change your *reliance on notifications to trigger an action* to *checking apps when you need to*. That's asynchronous work. You stop being responsive to, and governed by, time-based beeps and notifications that don't represent time at all—purely that someone else has completed their task.

The final habit is to do something about those emails that slip through the cracks. And, newsflash, there will be some. Only during the process of writing this book did I find out about Gated. But it's a must-have if you get flooded by spam emails.

When you sign up to Gated, you allow the email domains you want to get through and "gate" everyone else. Gating them responds to their emails saying you don't recognize their email addresses and, in an attempt to avoid spam, you'd like them to make a donation to a charity in order for their email to make it into your inbox.

Hiba Amin is a content marketer who was suffering from mailbox monotony. She brought Gated to my attention in her tweet:

"$12 raised passively towards Planned Parenthood so far because of Gated."

I was sold.

So far, I haven't raised any money. But I haven't had any unwanted emails either.

I've locked strangers out of my main inbox unless they donate to charity and it's such a sweet concept.

Glad to see it actually driving $$s!

Understanding that you don't have to be governed by technology goes a long way to gaining control of your day.

Up to this point, I've introduced some small habits to form and some large changes you can make to take steps to making your freelance business autonomous.

When you set yourself up to become an autonomous freelancer, you still come across the same issues as an ordinary freelancer.

Things like pricing, getting paid, and finding work don't disappear. But preparing yourself in such a way that they become much *much* easier is a great first step.

Would you believe me if I told you that I've never once pitched a client for work? They've all come to me.

Sounds pretty sweet, right? Trust me. It really is.

I hate sales. Even selling my own services. It's awkward, feels pushy, and isn't over quickly enough.

I realized this would be the case early on in my freelance career. I also made the correct assumption that it would take up considerable unbillable time if I got it wrong.

So, I got it right.

In the next few sections of this book, I'll introduce how you can do several things that made finding and landing customers a whole lot easier:

1. How to make work come to you
2. How to price work with autonomy in mind
3. How to put getting paid on autopilot

CHAPTER 4

HOW TO MAKE WORK COME TO YOU

I ask my Twitter audience questions like: "What's your least favorite part about writing?" and I get answers like "Finding clients". This makes me sad.

My query was to find out what people don't like about *writing*. The automatic association for some freelance writers is that writing is business.

When I ask questions like "What's your favorite part about writing?" I get answers like expression and freedom and other wonderful words that I also love about writing.

Likewise, when I join Twitter Chats about freelancing, the same topics come up time and again: finding clients is hard.

And, honestly, I don't get it.

Now, that might sound callous or arrogant. And maybe it is. Because, while I appreciate how hard it is to get new clients when you cold pitch and submit CVs, I can't get my head around why people don't deviate from this horrible process.

Albert Einstein said, "The definition of insanity is doing the same thing over and over and expecting different results."

So why do people persist in the process that's "hard, tiresome, boring, painful, arduous, mind-numbing, and demoralizing"?

The answer is: because it's habit. Remember that small word that causes so much pain or gain?

Let's do something about that habit.

I have secured customers from two avenues during my career as a freelance marketer. Note, I use the term "avenues" rather than channels or platforms. I'm not about to tell you to go all in on Twitter or start writing life-coaching posts on LinkedIn. Neither am I about to tell you to start writing long-form blog posts to try and rank on Google.

The two avenues that have bought me all my customers are:

1. Word of mouth referral.
2. Content promotion.

1 - Word of mouth referral

Word of mouth referrals are when someone literally recommends you to their colleagues, peers, friends, bosses, competitors, anyone.

I've had 25 customers in the last 5 years. To validate that word of mouth referrals not only exist but work, I've counted back which of those 25 have been word of mouth referrals.

Care to hazard a guess?

6* of those (24%) have come from word-of-mouth referrals. Actually, 3 of them were from the same person.

And that's only the referrals that became paying customers. Sometimes they weren't a good fit. And we've already touched on when it's okay to say no to new business.

*Editing note: I got 3 word of mouth referrals today. 2 within my niche and 1 under the blanket of digital marketing. These came from former customers and a person I network with online. Word of mouth is real, folks.

So, how do you get a word-of-mouth referral?

Other than having nice customers who do this naturally, it's a two-pronged approach to obtaining referrals:

1. Delivering great work.
2. Asking for referrals.

Delivering great work speaks for itself. If you provide late or below-par work, it's highly unlikely you're going to get a referral.

Not only does the work you deliver have to be great, but it must also be a good working experience for your client. If they have to chase you after delivery dates or you ignore feedback, you're no longer making your client's life easier. And, after all, that's why they hire you: you have a specialist skill they can't complete (or complete as well) in-house.

When you meet or exceed expectations time and again, referrals happen organically.

But there is still no harm in asking for a referral if you've delivered great work. For example, when growing one client's blog, we'd reached levels we could never have imagined. The impact on the business was so great that more than 90% of the pipeline could be attributed to work I'd completed. When the time came to reduce work with that particular client, I asked them if they knew anybody else who'd benefit from the work we'd done.

The result?

17 referrals.

And, no, that's not a typo.

My client was so thrilled with my work that they wanted to spread the word with peers, former colleagues, and investors.

Sure, not all 17 turned out to be anything. But they all have quality recommendations for when they do.

That said, it's hard to gain word of mouth referrals from existing customers only. And, what if you don't have many customers yet? That's where my second avenue comes in. Let's talk about content promotion.

2 - Content promotion

What's the first thing you do after you complete your work for a client?

Okay, after you breathe a sigh of relief, what *should* you do?

Promote your content.

Why?

Content promotion makes up the rest of the 76% of customers that have come to me and asked if I can do work for them.

By "content", let's assume I'm referring to whatever the output or deliverable is for your client. It may not be content in the traditional sense of consumable content marketing (videos, blogs, graphics, etc.) but you have provided someone with something. If you have no output to share, simply sharing that you've done something is great too. If you have a graph, chart, table, code snippet, behind-the-scenes photo, anything, it unlocks a passageway to being found online.

As well as the objection of having nothing to share (from freelancers who aren't writers or designers mostly), obtaining permission and dealing with NDAs are the next most common. I'll come to those shortly.

I'm forever surprised when I ask freelancers about their processes, and they don't include promotion outside of sharing on their favorite social media.

Don't get me wrong. Social media is great. As I was writing this book, I shared an ebook that I worked on 9 months ago on LinkedIn. Within an hour, I had a message in my DMs asking me to create the same for a new client. Since completing this book, I've completed that ebook. It netted me £7,500 ($9,000).

It doesn't always work that way. That's why you need to consistently be distributing your content.

A thorough content promotion process, which only needs to be bullets of where to share, can take eyeballs on your content and outputs from zero to hero. But eyeballs don't pay the bills. However, when the *right* people read your content, you stand a higher chance of getting business to come to you.

That's why content distribution is so hard. And why so many marketing teams deprioritize it. Finding the right places takes effort, time, and research. Writing a new blog post feels like you're contributing more. Creating a new infographic seems like everybody is busy. Creating new code when you haven't tested your previous shows your client you're efficient. But only on the front end. And, as any business-savvy person will tell you, it's what happens behind the scenes (or after publication or handover in the case of a freelancer) that makes businesses money. We're talking about optimization for search and promoting content in the right place.

To put that into context, I can attribute over $170,000 worth of work in the last 18 months to content promotion.

Over the last 5 years, I've collated where works, doesn't work, and only works for certain content, so I have a plan of where to share my content when it's ready to be released into the wild. Sure, I rely a lot on traffic from Google. But, in the example of one post in particular, I gained an extra 67% worth of views compared to just hitting publish and letting people find it on Google.

"Leaving dollars on the table" is an overused phrase in the marketing world. But, in the case of content distribution versus relying solely on SEO and a bit of luck, you're not only leaving dollars on the table (i.e. missing customers who'd find your work and approach you) but you're creating more work for yourself in terms of cold pitching and looking for gigs.

I promise you that promoting your content is a whole lot more validating too. Sharing something you made and getting feedback is invaluable. And don't get me started on the dopamine hit when you get a bunch of likes or someone shares something you created.

Yes, finding where and how to promote your content is hard. That's why I created my own checklist for others to use. Sure, you might not use all of them. But for less than $1 per tactic, I'd wager you spend a lot more unbilled time tiring yourself out applying for gigs.

You can download my content promotion checklist here: **bit.ly/ freelancepromochecklist**

And, if you do, you unlock a code for 33% off my blogging course too.

See what I did there? I just promoted my checklist and my course in my book!

Obtaining permission

The number one objection to promoting content that you've created is the fear that your customer won't let you. Let me be straight with you here. They wouldn't pay you if they didn't want people to see it.

As a business owner myself, when I commission someone to write a blog post or create a graphic for me, I want them to share it.

Why?

Because more people will see it!

If you can't get over this imaginary hurdle, there are some things you can do to:

1. Ask.
2. Do it anyway.

When you ask your client what their content promotion process is, you might even get some extra work too. If content distribution is a weakness of theirs, you might get a gig writing social media copy or tacking on some outreach time as a deliverable in your retainer.

If it's all taken care of in-house, a simple "I assume you'll want me to share it too?" puts you on the front foot. Why would they say no? You just offered to amplify the asset they're paying you to create.

Even in the case of ghostwriting, the act of sharing the post without publicly calling out you wrote it goes a long way. When someone reads it and thinks it's great, they'll ask you if you know the author. And that's you!

When you do it anyway, there are two outcomes:

1. Your client asks you to take it down.
2. Your client thanks you for sharing their content.

Use scenario judgment to gauge whether this is going to lose you a customer or gain you a fan. In most cases, however, if your name's on it, *not* promoting it is counterproductive to your freelance business.

Oh, but then there's the dreaded NDA…

Dealing with NDAs

NDA stands for Non-Disclosure Agreement. This means your client doesn't want you to disclose that you're working with them, a certain product, or part of their business. In the case of security or sensitive topics, this is fairly commonplace.

If "the brand" is the author of blog posts, you might see this too. But it's not the end of the world for promoting your content.

You have two options when a client proposes an NDA:
1. Challenge it.
2. Accept it.

If you challenge the NDA, there are two scenarios:
1. The client removes the NDA, and you continue your work (and are able to promote it later on).
2. The client insists on the NDA and you continue your work as they proposed.

The worst-case scenario is they say no. So there really is no harm in asking.

When you promote enough content, success, or metrics, you draw people toward you. Customers come to me because they want me to replicate the success I've had with previous customers.

One major thing that helps with drawing people towards you is being known for a specific niche. This could be industry-specific, asset-specific, or skill-specific.

In the next chapter, we take a deep dive into what being niche *actually* means and how you can go about finding your own.

CHAPTER 5

HOW TO FIND YOUR NICHE IN A NOISY ONLINE WORLD

When I give the advice of becoming an authority in a niche, freelancers ask me the same question over and over again:

"How do I find my niche?"

The answer here becomes rather convoluted. Hence, it's got its own chapter.

To find the right niche for you, we need to strip back what "being niche" means. There's often a rather blurry line.

What being niche means

Being niche means you specialize in a certain something. The more specific the better. And this is where it gets a little confusing.

People argue B2B SaaS is their niche. I argue they haven't found their niche.

Here's why...

B2B means business to business, right? And SaaS means software-as-a-service.

According to Statistica, there were over 25,000 companies listed as SaaS providers in 2022. I didn't think I needed to research how many B2B companies there were in the world.

My point here is that B2B SaaS is incredibly broad. The opposite of niche.

And while we're on the subject of SaaS, the real niche SaaS freelancers are those who understand the aaS element. As-a-service refers to the delivery model of said software (the first S).

Having spent 10 years in an industry that transitioned from on-premises hardware to SaaS, I have so many anecdotes and examples of what aaS really is. But I found Wikipedia had already done the hard work for me:

"As a service (AAS) is a business model in which something is being presented to a customer, either internal or external, as a service. As-a-Service offerings provide endpoints for customers/consumers to interface with which are usually API driven, but can commonly be controlled via a web console in a user's web browser."

We digress. But you understand my point, right?

Instead, being niche means being a specialist in a very particular thing. You could argue "specialty" is a better word to use. Instead of becoming niche in a particular area, marketing yourself as a specialist in writing code for CRM systems is clear and makes you stand out.

I'd hire the CRM-specializing coder if I wanted to write a new app that integrated with Salesforce instead of the B2B SaaS-er.

Let's define it then...

Being niche means you:

- Are a specialist in a specific area that requires in-depth expertise.
- Have demonstrable skills and/or highly relevant customer references.
- Can deliver a skill or asset using your experience, knowledge, and resources.

I left that definition for six weeks before coming back to it and I don't think I want to change anything.

But to make sure I wasn't blinkered in my definition, I asked fellow freelancers on Twitter what being niche meant to them.

Jason Patterson, a freelance content marketer, defines being niche as "means all the clients in your industry know your name."

Harshala Chavan, a freelance writer, says: "Being niche, especially as a writer, means your expertise in that subject is as good as the big 4 consultancies. You are capable of stating and drawing unique insights about that subject and presenting it in simple language on your own."

Dan Richards-Dan, a science and research communications freelancer, points out the benefits for both parties: "For me - I get to work for the sector I love and charge a rate according to my specialist knowledge. For my clients, higher value not just for my skills and experience, but because I can span cross-sector boundaries in ways their own staff can't."

Cici Asanga, a freelance health writer, took another angle when responding. I loved it too much not to include it: "It means more referrals and recommendations. People know what you do and can see you do it well so when anyone wants that service you come to mind. It means knowing people that are likely to value what you do. It means better rates."

What being niche doesn't mean

There's enormous confusion over what niche *actually* means. Especially in the content marketing world.

So let's remove ourselves from that world for a second.

When you Google "niche", here are the top 3 answers:

1. Denoting products, services, or interests that appeal to a small, specialized section of the population.
2. A niche is a place or position that's particularly appropriate for someone or something, especially due to being very specific and different from others.
3. A job, position, or place that is very suitable for someone.

Key phrases to extract from these are **appeal, specialized, appropriate, specific, different from others,** and **suitable.**

I thought it would be fun to make a sentence out of these. Here's what I came up with...

To appeal to specific clients and appear different from others, you must be specialized in a suitable niche to qualify as the appropriate candidate.

A bit wordy. If I had to simplify, it'd be something like: you gotta get good at something specific.

Back in the content marketing world, a good example of niche content creation is Case Study Buddy by Joel Klette. Joel's service quite clearly provides case studies. Specifically, B2B case studies. You might remember that I poo-pooed the idea that B2B is a niche. But it's the service in this case that is niche. Joel doesn't write blog posts for clients (through this service at least), only case studies. A great example of doubling down on something people need, you are good at, and is in high demand.

A bad example of niche content creation is those who say that they "can write anything". While I don't object to generalist writers (there is a great need for budget writers who can research almost anything and produce a near-end product), their decision not to focus on one industry, skill, or specialty means their rate is often set by clients and the potential pool of applicants is incredibly large.

A note on working outside your niche...

Being niche doesn't mean that you can *only* work in that niche. That's something that often gets confused too.

Just because I write about business communications technology, it doesn't mean I can't ever work in another industry. In fact, this year you could say I extended my niche. I'm writing for several asynchronous video clients. My background in video conferencing is highly relevant but so is my attitude to and my belief of working asynchronously. Just because those clients aren't recognized as business communications vendors, it doesn't mean I don't want to work with them (or them me).

Removing myself totally from my niche, I wrote a blog post on SMS marketing a few months back. I was ahead of my workload, hadn't yet started this book, and someone reached out looking for a freelance writer recommendation. Selfishly, I said I actually had the day free tomorrow so I wrote the blog post and collected the paycheck for something outside my niche.

While the subject matter wasn't within my niche, it was being successful in my niche that pointed the client to me.

Here's a blog post I wrote for Superpath.co as I was writing this book. It's highly relevant to this section so I couldn't not include it.

How Freelancers Can Narrow Their Niche and Earn More Money

I'm a freelance content marketer and I am *extremely* niche.

Some people see this as a bad thing. They think it narrows your potential client base and reduces income opportunities.

While the former is true, the latter couldn't be further from the truth.

I find that a lot of people don't understand what niche actually means. Maybe that's where the problem lies.

I only work with unified communications and contact center vendors because I have 10 years' experience on the product side. That means I have an advantage over 10,000s of marketers when it comes to knowing the products, audience, pain points, inner workings, etc.

That's niche.

In this article, I share five tips that I shared in the Superpath Slack group when asked for my best advice when it comes to choosing a niche.

Before that, let's spend a little time dispelling those horrible myths about freelancing.

Niche freelancers have a smaller client pool

A smaller client pool than *the rest of the world*, sure.

It might seem scary at first. But narrowing down your client pool **is a good thing.**

Here's why…

When you focus on one industry, type of work, or subset of that work, you become an expert in this particular area.

For example, I write about unified comms and contact centers. Almost exclusively.

My customers are unified comms providers like Cisco and contact center providers like Nextiva.

With 13 years' experience working with and writing for these vendors, do you think they prefer hiring generalist writers who don't know about their tech, audience, or brand?

Absolutely not.

They want to find and hire someone who's been there, done that, and bought the t-shirt.

And they'll pay more for it.

Assuming you don't choose something super niche that has two potential customers fighting against each other (I can't think of any of these, and I've spent a long time doing so), there's no such thing as too niche. And you don't need to worry about having a client pool too small.

Also, just because I operate in the unified comms and contact center space, it doesn't mean I *can't* write for anyone else.

This year (2022) alone, I've written for Semrush, Logo.com, and Better Proposals.

And, hey, here I am writing for Superpath!

Niche freelancers reduce their income opportunities

Smaller pool = less chance of income?

Incorrect.

Smaller pool = higher chance of being hired in that pool.

Add to that the tailored portfolio you have built or are building.

You have a custom batch of work ready to showcase to your potential customers.

Here's a scenario I find myself in all the time. Sometimes I'm the hirer and sometimes I'm the hiree.

When I'm the hiree

"Please can you send a sample of your work for me to review."

"Sure, here's something I wrote that ranks #1 on Google for your top competitor. How about we do the same for you?"

It doesn't have to be that forward but you get the point.

And it's sure better than this…

When I'm the hirer

"Please can you send a sample of your work for me to review. Ideally, it's relevant to our audience and showcases you know the tech we work with."

"Sorry, all I have is this generic post about blah blah blah."

The first example gets me hired every single time.

The second example is from my real life where I get pitched by 100s of writers a year who know nothing about the topics, tech, industry, problems, audience, or pretty much anything I write about.

Yes, everybody has to start somewhere. And if this is the start of your niche process, make sure your answer reflects that.

If you're going through the narrowing your niche process, here are five tips to nail it.

5 tips to successfully narrow your niche

Disclaimer: My process was ready-made for me. I have 10 years' experience on the product side of things so maybe I'm not the best person to comment on choosing from the beginning.

If I was to start again, I would choose something that:

1 - Is a high-value industry with clear road to increasing market over time

You gotta get paid, right?

If you're at the point in your career where you're choosing your niche, you might as well make it a well-paid one.

If products or solutions are high-ticket, the marketing efforts behind them must be high-ticket too.

Some of my clients sell packages to enterprises worth millions per year.

They know a $100 copywriter likely won't produce the same results as a $1,000 copywriter with years of experience in their niche.

Finding an industry where the marketing efforts reflect what's being sold is key if you want to earn *great money* as a freelancer.

And not just great money today.

Think about whether the products and service will:

- Be relevant in five years' time
- Increase in demand over time
- Launch other products and services
- Generate a market of genuine interest indefinitely
- Integrate with other products where you can expand

If you don't consider this, you might get a big paycheck for 2 years then have to start all over again.

You only have to look as far as the crypto marketers getting $$$ in Ethereum and Bitcoin, only for the market to crash and work to dry up.

Sure, it might come back, but what are they doing right now?

Reading this post?

2 - Excites me to go to work

There are only so many ways to write how great a client's email automation software is, for example.

You're still just sending emails.

If this is your thing, though, you could branch out into other types of automation software. Becoming an automation specialist opens the door to tons of opportunities.

The same is true for almost any industry.

Start by writing a list of what you get excited to write about.

Remove the bias of what you *actually* write about and note down what you'd *like* to write about.

This might be a *type* of work rather than an industry too. Joel Klettke, for example, excels (and I assume enjoys) when writing B2B case studies. So that's the niche Joel has chosen.

When you've got a list of five things, note down five potential customers.

You've started narrowing your niche already.

3 - Is a rewarding environment to be in

Are industry analysts, commentators, readers, going to share my work or collaborate with me (or is it a closed-off and stuffy industry)?

Maybe this one is just an ego boost. But it also helps build your personal brand.

If other industry folk enjoy your content, they might one day hire you.

Since becoming a marketer for unified comms companies, I've started my business, UC Marketing. I was known as "the UC marketer" in the industry so it made sense to name my business this.

It also embeds me firmly within my niche. And I do so because it's rewarding.

When people enjoy my content, they share it. They reach out to say well done. They recommend me when others need help with marketing.

Choose a niche that triggers a positive emotion when you deliver your output.

It could be a blog post, an infographic, or custom code. Just make sure it's rewarding.

4 - I know enough about it to hit the ground running

Saheed Hassan, a fellow freelance writer, posed this question the day before I started writing this post.

"Forget your current clients—let's assume you're just starting. Of course, you've got some samples in your portfolio—how will you raise $3k before month end?"

My answer here is to choose a niche you're proficient in.

That doesn't mean you know how to use a laptop so you become a laptop reviewer. But it might mean you have an engineering degree so you choose manufacturing and welding as your bespoke topic set.

My biggest advice to freelancers looking to find their niche is:

Write about what you know.

If you're not a writer, adjust that phrase slightly.

That's not just how I became a high-paid freelance marketer, it's *why I became* a high-paid freelance marketer.

I have 10 years' experience working with the products and customers that I now provide marketing services for.

This means I don't have to learn something new every time I pitch or land a client. And it means I lean on my first-hand experience and knowledge to produce high-quality content in a quicker turnaround time.

The benefit of that?

I can slot in more work (or have time off)! And I can charge a higher rate because I know the value I offer my clients.

When choosing your niche, write about what you know, folks.

5 - Is an industry I can continue learning about as it evolves

While I advocate choosing a niche where you're a subject matter expert (or at least a subject matter intermediate), I'm a forever learner.

What does that mean, then?

A forever learner is someone who values continuous learning.

Learning didn't end at college for me.

In my career, I've picked up the following formal and informal qualifications:

- Prince2 Project Management
- Business Analysis Practitioner
- Advanced Google Analytics
- Pragmatic Marketing Level 3
- HubSpot Social Media Marketing

- Slack Basics
- Getting Started with Zoom Chat

I've read 100+ books on business, writing, and marketing.

I've also learned about 100+ products with 1,000+ features in my industry. And I've met new audiences that include small businesses, mid-size businesses, enterprises, frontline workforces, desk-based workers, IT admins, CEOs, CTOs, CeverythingOs, mobile workers, consultants, and plenty more.

The combination of these, driven by my desire to be the best in my niche, means I make sure I'm always learning *something* because my niche is always evolving.

If my chosen niche was stagnant, I would be too.

Your first step to finding your niche as a freelancer

My parting advice is the *very first thing you should do*...

Start by writing a list of what you get excited to write about.

(Or code, design, strategize, etc.)

And do it by hand.

Switch off from the online world and spend some time working out where you fit.

You can trust me; I'm a freelance content marketer and I am *extremely* niche.

End of article.

Becoming the go-to person in your niche

For work to come to you, you need to become *known*. Not famous. Not flamboyant. But known.

I'm known as the content marketer who works with unified comms companies. I actually don't know anybody else who specializes in this. The alternatives are in-house content marketing, generalist agencies, and not doing any content marketing. If you have bandwidth in-house, go for it. If you don't, don't hire the agency that has never heard of your product, doesn't know your audience, and probably doesn't care. Hire the niche freelancer instead. The person who lives and breathes this stuff and is also a marketer.

So, how do you get to this stage? It takes hard work. It takes experience. Then it takes smart work and smart marketing.

I talk to people about earning more money through freelancing and the first thing I mention is finding a niche. They immediately say something broad like "B2B eCommerce" so we have the discussion about what niche really means and how going narrow correlates with earning more.

When you've established yourself as a niche freelancer, you need to get word out.

We're talking about distribution and promotion here. But we're also talking about delivery.

When you deliver high-quality work, people talk about it. (See the chapter on word-of-mouth referrals.)

When you do this well and consistently (both, not either), you create an almost viral impact where people will keep knocking your door for you to help them out. Sure, not every lead will convert immediately, but that's marketing. Raising awareness = raising your profile. The higher your profile, the more likely people are to come to you.

So where to get started so people know what you do?

If you don't make it clear, people won't know.

On your Twitter bio, LinkedIn account, your personal website, wherever you have a presence, write what you do. Make it super clear and free of jargon.

When there was talk of everybody leaving Twitter in November 2022, I put this thread together explaining how I optimized my LinkedIn profile to generate $100,000s of inbound revenue...

1 - *Your profile*

Treat this as your landing page.

Tell a visitor exactly what you do.

There should be no doubt you're an ABC that does XYZ in the 123 industry when someone reads your profile.

Keep your copy simple and jargon-free.

2 - *Your profile picture*

Have one.

Make it professional.

3 - *Your first line on your About section*

LinkedIn shows the smallest amount of text here so people either click "see more" or they click away.

Add the most important part of your profile here.

4 - *Your USP*

There are 10,000s of people who do similar things to you, so make sure you stand out.

Include:

- your niche
- your best accomplishment
- your biggest clients
- your portfolio link

5 - *Your unfair advantage*

This is what makes people reach out.

Literally tell them why you're better than the next person they're about to click on.

6 - *Your presence*

If your profile looks unused, potential customers and connections will ignore you.

You don't have to go all in and post 50 times a day - but commenting and posting SOMETHING is at least keeping up appearances.

7 - *Your optimized headline*

People find you on LinkedIn almost like they do on Google.

If your profile contains the words they use, you will appear.

Think about the right combination of words you want to be found for (and how many other people are doing the same).

7 (**a**) - You might be a B2B writer but you're not going to be found if you type that.

There are 125,000+ B2B writers on LinkedIn.

Instead, list your type of writing, your industry, and keywords.

Mine are super niche:

Content marketing in unified comms | Freelance content strategist and content writer for unified comms and contact center

7 (**b**) Yes, that means I won't be found when people search for a B2B writer.

But it also propels me to the top when people search unified comms content marketing or contact center writer.

Tune into your target audience and use their terminology.

8 - Your topics

Once you've optimized with your niche and desired job title, LinkedIn lets you add hashtags to show what you talk about.

Use this the other way around.

Optimize for the topics people follow that you'd like to be found for.

9 - Your connections

If you add people, LinkedIn scans to understand common audiences. As a result, you're presented with similar connections.

Think about this the other way around; whose connection suggestions do you want to be on?

Surround yourself with similar connections.

10 - Your experience

Make it easy to scan. It's not a CV.

Add a description to your most recent job then list out the others so it's easy to flick through.

Add samples per job/gig if relevant.

Let people see your work so they know how great you are.

11 - Your featured section

Pin posts that are important and you want people to see.

It could be a portfolio or CV link.

I showcase the articles I'm most proud of.

12 - Your LinkedIn Groups

When you find active groups that aren't full of spam, they can be a gold mine.

I hang out in industry-specific groups to gather ideas, offer help, and promote my content.

You'll be surprised how many DMs I get saying "I saw you in ABC LinkedIn group."

This thread was specific to LinkedIn but the same principles apply to any platform.

If you make it easy for people to find the person/service they're looking for, they have a much better chance of finding you when you happen to be that exact person/service.

Over time, and depending on your appetite, you might even become the person directing your niche. Araminta Robertson was a freelance marketer working with FinTech clients. Now, she's the person everyone goes to for advice, jobs, research, and just about anything related to marketing in FinTech.

You don't have to set up an entire community, run a podcast, or a newsletter. (Though these are all great ideas.) But every interaction you have with someone about your niche service or industry is brand awareness. It might be as small as a Twitter DM or a share of your article. It might be a $50,000 project. No matter the size of the interaction, you are becoming the person to go to for your niche.

Reminder: During your promotion/marketing phases, communicate how you prefer to work. Tell other people about the benefits of having fewer meetings. Sing the praises of asynchronous communications. Build expectations for your next customer.

This can be a tweet when you get a task done using a specific tool. It might be when you finish at 10am because you've nailed your process. Whatever it is, setting the tone in public (and to your potential next client) saves you the time and energy of explaining why you want to work in such a manner. You start to attract like-minded customers who respect how you work and let you get on with doing what you do best.

What sounds more perfect than that? Actually, how about increasing your revenue? And how about doing that without working more?

Sounds too good to be true, doesn't it? I thought it was. Until I learned it wasn't.

CHAPTER 6

HOW TO PRICE WORK WITH AUTONOMY IN MIND

I've spoken to hundreds of freelancers who say they underprice themselves. This baffles me. They literally know they are underpricing themselves but aren't doing anything about it.

When I dig deeper, I find reasons are almost always related to confidence and imposter syndrome.

One of the biggest benefits of working asynchronously is that you can present your pricing in an email, a deck, a spreadsheet, or a proposal *without* having to ask for money face-to-face (or camera-to-camera).

When quoting for custom projects, or defining the price of any of your services, commons ways to do this are:

- Per word
- Per hour
- Per day

All these restrict you to time-based activities. Not autonomous. Without knowing it, you probably spend (and lose) time keeping track of what you did that hour, filling out timesheets, and sending lots of small invoices.

Stop using time-based billing as soon as you can.

You might not want to rock the boat with existing customers, and that's fine. Sometimes the relationship is worth more than trying to earn more money from that single client. But when you advertise your services or provide your next quote, move to a better method of pricing...

Ideally, you want to move to:

- Retainers
- Fixed pricing
- Value-based pricing

Retainers are ideal for long-term engagements. Especially when your work doesn't directly reflect a deliverable. For example, Mio pays me the same fee every month as we build a content marketing machine. There is a shared benefit of not charging them per item and there is a shared benefit of committing set time per month. If I was only writing blog posts for them, it would make sense for me to charge them *per blog post*. But a lot of the work I do surrounds distribution, brand awareness, and SEO. It's hard to make these tangible, so this way I benefit from knowing I can run experiments and test new things safe in the knowledge that my fee isn't dependent on everything that eventually leads up to success. That's me genuinely providing a service; and where **retainers** are great. Generally, we set a high rate for a short retainer and the price comes down to an almost full-time-reflective rate if you're working that much.

If you provide one-off or regular products, like a blog post or an infographic, **fixed pricing** makes much more sense. Your client knows exactly what they're paying and what's included.

An example might be that you are asked to design an ebook. If your cost for 1 x ebook is $500 then everyone knows where they stand. Usually, you generate this price based on how long it takes you to complete the deliverable + time for contingency. (Always allow yourself this protection.) 20% is a good rule of thumb that I've seen a lot of successful freelancers use.

At the same time, though, you must be aware that this ebook is going to generate thousands, maybe even hundreds of thousands of revenue. And if you know this, your client knows this too.

This is where **value-based pricing** comes in.

Before we cover how to work out value-based pricing, let's touch on what you're not going to include:

Details.

Obviously, you'll share some details but you can template this. You specialize in a certain skill so include those slides/documents. You specialize in a certain industry so include that too.

But you're not going to include every specific activity.

Why?

Because, for most freelance projects, you can't account for how long they will take. While you might do a lot of the same thing, every project is different somehow.

A content marketing strategy for one client might take me 5 days. But for a larger client with different needs, more resources, and a larger budget, it could take me 5 *weeks*.

Inside this deliverable of a content marketing strategy, there are lots of small tasks you'll conduct too. Your client doesn't need to know you might spend 5 hours on calls with their product managers or 3 hours searching competitors' sites online.

They need to know how much the content marketing strategy is going to cost.

Here, you're better off dictating the scope too. I always lay out what is included in the project fee e.g. copy and one round of edits. But I also include what's not included. Some of these could be optional extras, like social media copy to promote your blog post or any other service you offer.

When you do this, you increase the opportunity for extra work from the same client.

Important: don't let this detract from your main goal: signing the contract.

Take a judgment call whether including optional extras is a good move or not. In the example of social media copy, check on LinkedIn whether your client already has a social media manager.

Even if you don't have other services or products to add here, creating a clear line between what is in scope and what is out-of-scope is always a good move. If you're not going to source unique quotes or can't access product screenshots, call this out and make it clear in black and white.

Side note: customers will love it when you provide the entire service. It's a pet hate of mine when writers send me a blog post draft and it's just words. As Andy Crestodina, founder of Orbit Media, and my content marketing mentor, says:

"I would never post an article without at least one compelling visual, an expert contributor quote, and genuine first-hand research."

Whatever you choose to include or not include, make it extremely clear.

Use your judgment to decide when it's the right time to use retainers vs fixed price vs value-based. You might even find that fixed price merges into value-based and your commonly-bought services end up at a higher price than you previously charged.

But what is the right amount?

This is one of the questions that freelancers get hung up on. And this is where owning your niche comes into its own.

If I'm hiring someone to write an article that *any writer* could write, there's a set fee associated. For example, for one of my clients where I am the editor, I offer a flat fee of $300 per article. These articles earn the business more than $300 per month but that doesn't mean we need to pay $3,000 for it. This is because the pool for general content writing is LARGE. It's a race to the bottom on price for generalist copywriters who don't need much experience in a certain technology to write some of our articles.

At the other end of the spectrum, I write or commission incredibly specialist articles where I need someone who has hands-on experience with the technology, has worked in enterprise environments, and interviewed people in charge of million-dollar budgets. Someone who is niche to that topic.

In the latter scenario, when you are one of few, *you* are in control of the pricing. This is where I made the majority of my money in 2022—not retainers.

It wasn't through volume either. I wrote less in 2022 than 2020 or 2021 yet I earned more money.

With the majority of my clients, they don't need convincing that craft is something worth paying for. That's not necessarily a reflection on me, other than that I choose to work with clients who understand that content marketing is effective and worth doing well.

In another world, I might have to sell the premise of content marketing *as well as selling myself*. This is something you don't want to get into and will immediately devalue your service. I distanced myself from potential clients who didn't fully understand what I do and why my price might be higher than their previous freelancer. Sure, I could remind them that they got rid of their previous freelancer. But it's a losing battle for the most part.

I avoid these conversations altogether by making my pricing available in the public domain. By that, I mean my popular services have their own landing page on my website and I send people there.

This does three things that you'd otherwise spend your time on:

1. Selling your type of service as well as *your* service.
2. Filtering out people who can't afford you.
3. Remove the pricing surprise *after* you've spent time talking to them.

If you have a price list publicly available, you avoid the awkwardness of unexpected prices completely. Yes, some freelancers find it awkward asking for money. I still do sometimes.

There are two ways to get around that:
1. Make your pricing available in the public domain (and send people there).
2. Only do it via written communications.

Unless you're a seasoned sales pro, you'll likely be on the back foot anytime someone challenges you in a live call. So, protect yourself. When you do end up discussing pricing face-to-face, make phrases like "let me confirm that for you after the call" or "I'll get you that by the end of the day" part of your in-call vocabulary.

Or, in a perfect world, they already know. Because you made your pricing public.

There's a big argument *not* to make your pricing public. I asked for some of these on my Twitter with the plan to include the best ones in this book.

But you'll find this section empty as nobody could give me anything that didn't translate as "Because I've always done it this way".

My personal experience proves that having your pricing public makes your sales process more efficient. But I do advocate custom pricing for custom projects. And you should make this clear online too. Or, in most cases, you won't have to. Lots of people buy blog posts or ebooks from me. But lots also engage me for strategy work. And this is hard to price. Sure, I could productize it and make every content marketing strategy $25,000. But every business is different and will have different deliverables based on its marketing maturity. In this example, I've made a startup content marketing strategy product (which you can buy for $25,000) but other businesses need custom pricing and deliverables.

So that's pricing. What happens when a client agrees your rate?

It's time for them to pay up. In a perfect world, this would be the full amount. Then you could be safe and happy in the knowledge that you can focus on your craft.

In some cases, when you have great clients and/or a reputation that allows you to command your fee upfront, this is standard practice. With my two latest clients, they both paid upfront without batting an eyelid. These were clients in my niche and I already established a relationship with them. The trust has already been gained. They know I will deliver.

If they don't say yes to this, or you feel you are too early in your career to ask, you must ask for a deposit upfront. 50% is not unreasonable. This way you split the risk between freelancer and client.

There is only one exception here. That's when both parties sign a contract to confirm you will get paid X amount on delivery of your service or on X day per month.

If you don't get a deposit or sign a contract, this is a red flag. Your client is not making any commitment and has transferred all the risk to you.

Ask yourself these questions:
- What happens if they go bust overnight?
- What happens if they pause the project?
- What happens if they find someone cheaper?

The answer in all cases is that you have spent time and effort creating something but aren't getting paid for it.

Some people will argue that they trust their clients and feel bad for asking for a contract. This is rubbish. There is no reasonable argument for not securing a deposit or signing a contract.

If you don't have your own contract to send to clients, use this template I made here: **bit.ly/freelancer-template** or extract the best bits from the next few pages...

Contract Agreement

between

CLIENT NAME

and

YOUR NAME OR COMPANY NAME

Your company name: **Service Agreement**

Your name or company (also known as "Contractor") will provide Client name, a corporation having its registered office in CLIENT ADDRESS (also known as "Client") with content marketing services as to the specifications detailed below.

Contract in effect beginning: TODAY'S DATE

Services

Contractor will provide the following mutually agreed upon services until the project has completed:

Services	Included In Project
Add every service you provide here and tick off the ones you are going to provide on this contract	
Add every service you provide here	
Add every service you provide here	
Add every service you provide here	
Add every service you provide here	
Add every service you provide here	

The Contractor will provide 3 x long-form blog posts per month at a rate of XXX per deliverable.

Payment

Client will pay the Contractor **XXXX** on the XXX of every month of the engagement following production of an invoice sent to CLIENT EMAIL, or the next banking day should it fall on a weekend or national holiday. The minimum engagement term is XXXX.

Payment after that date will incur a late fee of £0.44 per day on the outstanding amount as well as a compensation fee of £70.

The Client shall reimburse all reasonable expenses properly and necessarily incurred by the Contractor in respect of the provision of the services as per the Contractor's statutory right to claim interest (at 8% over the Bank of England base rate) and compensation for debt recovery costs under the Late Payment legislation because the Contractor was not paid according to the agreed credit terms.

Changes

Client and Contractor agree to changes requiring no more than 10% of the overall project efforts and output during the phase of the project.

Further changes are chargeable and subject to a new Contractor project agreement.

Legal

The Contractor can't guarantee that work will be completely error-free and is not liable to you or any third party for damages, including lost profits, lost savings, or other incidental, consequential, or special damages, even if the Client advises the Contractor of them. If any provision of this contract shall be unlawful, void, or for any reason unenforceable, then that provision shall be deemed severable from this contract and shall not affect the validity and enforceability of any remaining provisions.

Copyright

Client will own the copyright for all material created under this agreement. The contractor can showcase sample works from this project as portfolio pieces.

Testimonial

Client agrees for logo usage on Contractor website and marketing materials. Client agrees to provide reference quote for usage on Contractor website and marketing materials.

Client agrees to terms and policies specified above:

Signature: _____

Name & Title: _____

Date: _____

Accepted by Contractor:

_____

Name & Title: _____

Date: _____

Then, to make your client's life easier and increase the chance of signature, use an electronic signature platform like DocuSign so they don't need to print it out and sign it.

In this example contract, I've included things like showcasing other services to boost the chance of getting extra work from the same client. This is totally optional.

The alternative to this, and something I always check, is to sign *their* contract. Always ask about this first. The last thing you want to do is spend an hour making sure your contract is perfect, only for them to say they have one already. Trust me. I've been there and done that for you.

All these tips are well and good *if* you end up delivering what you priced. But what happens when a client asks you for something outside of what you planned to deliver?

Protecting yourself from free work and scope creep

Your proposal is just that. It's not an estimate. It's your proposed rate for the work you are going to deliver. The costs will not vary if you deliver what has been agreed.

If they need something else, it's going to cost them. If you increase the scope, you increase the cost.

Junior freelancers feel bad about this. Until they realize it's hurting their business.

Freelancers feel bad when they get it wrong. And that's only right. But by detailing your scope and deliverables early on, you save yourself from this conundrum.

The goal should always be to provide a price with scope that doesn't need to be altered. Even if it's your client's fault, your client has a negative experience going back and forth.

Allowing scope creep removes your autonomy. You no longer have the freedom to start other work or side projects when you get ahead of your workload. Scope creep is the nemesis of every freelancer.

Protect yourself.

I hear from freelancers all the time that they did this but sometimes they *still* end up agreeing to out of scope work without asking for more money.

Instead of falling into this trap, use these phrases to reinforce your stance. Note that they all start with yes. This is to begin the conversation in a positive way (rather than just saying no).

- Yes, we can add that to the scope of the project. Attached is the invoice for the amendments.

- Yes, I can do that for you. I'll need to create a change to the scope of work and send you a revised proposal.
- Yes, let's create a new project for the revisions and I'll send you a new invoice later today.

Using these phrases makes your point clear. You *can* do what they're asking. But they *will* cost because they weren't in the original scope.

If you fail to capture scope changes as billable items, you'll spend all the time you earned applying other productivity tips on free work. Doesn't sound very autonomous, does it?

When you nail scope creep avoidance, you can continue your freelance growth.

In a blog I wrote for Better Proposals, I shared 5 changes freelancers can make to earn more money. While the focus of this book is not to make more money freelancing, becoming autonomous as a freelancer is frequently synonymous with earning more money.

Some of the points I share to make more money go hand in hand with freelance autonomy. Hence, I'm sharing the entire blog post with you now:

How much is your craft worth? More than what you're currently charging?

Yep, we thought so too.

You hear stories about freelance writers earning six and even seven figures per year. So, how do you join this elite group?

There is no get-rich-quick scheme but there are some things you can change to see almost immediate gains.

In this post, we address how freelancers can make more money without working more hours.

The answer lies within five small changes you can make to the way you operate your freelance business.

1. Pricing freelance projects

The most common freelance pricing model is billing for your time in your business proposals. Your day rate or your hourly rate.

Now, there is nothing wrong with billing your time if your clients are paying you a lot of money. For example, Erin Balsa, a B2B SaaS content marketer, bills $1,000 per day.

But if you're not making that kind of money, changing your pricing model might be an easy win.

Olly Meakings is a freelance full-stack marketer who started freelancing on £20 per hour. Today, he's more than 10x-ed his hourly rate for freelance work. When asked how he achieved this, he says:

"Well, I just kept asking for more. Like the famous Oliver, I suppose."

This is sound advice in itself. If a client says yes to your rates, that's a qualification that your rate is okay. And it gives you the permission and incentive to ask for more with your next client.

Bullish freelancers will say to keep upping your rates until a client says no. In fact, Brooklin Nash, a freelance content marketer, built up his income to over $300k/year between 2019 and 2021 with this mantra.

Here's how he did it:

– Just charge more.

"Honestly. Simple as that. It sounds simple, but any freelancer who has increased their rates can tell you it's scary. What if they say no? What if I never get work again? It's a difficult mental hurdle to get over. But remember: it's just mental. It's all in your head. Over the course of two years, I raised my rates with existing clients twice and increased my rates for new clients every time I signed a new contract. If you're doing great work and you've been consistent for your clients, let me tell you: you're worth it."

Productizing your work

But it's not this mentality that earns Olly the most money. It's changing his pricing model.

Rather than spending all his time on hourly work, he's packaged what he does best into a product. On RoastMyLandingPage, Olly provides informed feedback on how businesses can improve their landing pages to earn more conversions.

Olly is not charging for time here. He is charging for the value of the product he creates. While it may take him less than an hour to roast some landing pages, his customers earn tens of thousands of dollars more by implementing his changes.

2. Finding a routine that works for you

The first half of the word "freelance" is free. So, routine isn't something you have to nail down immediately (or ever). But finding your optimum way of working unlocks the door to productivity levels you didn't know you could reach.

The goal here is to find autonomy in your work.

For example, a day interrupted by dropping the kids off at school could be avoided by not starting your focus time until that task is complete. One focused hour is often better than three hours with several interruptions.

A better example is removing temptations. More specifically, changing the temptations to rewards. Try out this gamification process and tailor it to something manageable for you.

- Acknowledge the temptation
- Set it as a goal for when you complete a task
- Increase the reward as the day goes on or as the task size/value increases

You don't have to use this process, of course. It's just one example of a routine powered by reward. Play around with your routine and track what makes you most productive.

When you complete more in a day, you can bill more clients (without working more hours).

3. Reducing admin time

Lots of freelancers cite admin time as a blocker for taking on more clients. This could be self-marketing, accounting, or any other business task.

These are important. After all, you are a business as well as an employee.

As a result of changing your pricing model and your routine, you may find you have spare time to dedicate to admin. But that doesn't mean you have to.

There are two approaches you can take to reduce admin time as a freelancer:

- Dedicate a day/time slot for admin.
- Do your admin immediately.

Option 1 is obvious. You could make Friday your admin day. Update your website, send your invoices, reach out for case studies.

Option 2 means completing those tasks as and when they crop up.

For example, when you complete a project with a client, write a testimonial for them to approve instead of just saying thanks. When you get that approval, add it to your site there and then. Don't put it on your to-do list with your other non-billable items. Get. It. Done.

Another easy win is sending your invoice as soon as work is complete. This might mean reviewing your contract templates to say so. Most customers will be okay with this. In enterprises with lots of other businesses, it's not so easy – but you won't know unless you ask.

If your client doesn't pay? Don't spend time on time-consuming emails. Set your invoicing software to send automatic chasers when the payment date passes.

Small changes add up throughout the year. You could save weeks of admin time and spend time on billable work.

If it is your accounting that's eating up your time, hire an accountant.

Use the formula of:

Time spent on accounting tasks x Your hourly rate = Cost of accounting
Cost of accountant

For example, if you spend 20 hours per year on accounting tasks and your hourly rate is $50 then your cost of accounting is $1,000 per year.

If the cost of hiring an accountant to do these tasks is less than $1,000 then it's worth hiring an accountant. You get your 20 hours back and can fill this time with billable work.

4. Increasing billable work

When you've saved all that time on internal admin, what will you do with all your spare time?

There's no right or wrong answer here.

You could opt to take every Friday off or finish at 2 PM each day. There's absolutely nothing wrong with that.

But if you've saved time and your goal is to increase your earnings, use it wisely.

You could:

- Write a book
- Create a course
- Take on a new client
- Dip into affiliate marketing
- Increase your workload with an existing client

- Start a course/qualification that can help expand your product set

5. Expanding your product set

In The Four-Hour Work Week by Tim Ferris, you learn how selling a product means you can work less by selling things. What the book doesn't cover is what things to sell and how to find or create them.

Often, you can expand the services you offer and package them as a product. If you have the skills, why not market them?

Brooklin Nash (the freelancer earning $300k a year above), says you need to bring more to the table.

"The biggest jump in my income came when I started helping clients with earlier stages of content strategy and planning.

Instead of writing SEO articles based on an extensive brief, I ran the organic research, planned out the editorial calendar, and then executed it. Moreover, instead of turning pages of interview notes into a case study, I started running the interviews—or at least made it clear that I could run with a customer transcript and nothing else.

Last but not least, instead of writing thought leadership articles based on existing topics, I started interviewing leadership and then turned that into a laundry list of topics that could work for category education.

Clients usually outsource work to you for one of two reasons: they don't have time for something or they don't have the expertise for something. The first is a good place to start; the second is a great place to grow."

If you don't have these skills today, invest in yourself. Take the course. Read the book. Ask a peer.

£100 invested in yourself today could mean £10,000 earned a year.

How freelancers can command better rates

In summary, the changes freelancers can make to command better rates are:

- Pricing freelance projects
- Finding a routine that works for you
- Reducing admin time
- Increasing billable work
- Expanding your product set

You don't need to make all these changes at once. In fact, it is strongly recommended you pick the one that appeals most. If you're motivated by one more than the other, start here.

Changing how you work is hard work. Humans are the most resistant animals to change on the planet.

But when you gain momentum, there's no stopping you.

CHAPTER 7

HOW TO PUT GETTING PAID ON AUTOPILOT

In the last chapter, we covered contracts and deposits. When you've sent/requested those, you might think the ball is on your client's side of the court.

That's only the case if you made it very easy to get paid.

How do you do this?

I've hired (or tried to hire) freelancers who are damn near impossible to pay. I've also been the freelancer trying his hardest to get paid by a giant conglomerate that took over 100 days to pay me. I've also been slap bang in the middle when I've sent an invoice and it's been paid in the suggested time.

First of all, make it easy to get paid. This means you have a bank account that anyone can pay. And accept any currency. If you're refusing to be paid in $$$ because you're in the UK, you're making life harder for yourself.

Recent history shows that you'd have actually been better off (financially) if you accepted dollars in the UK. Overall history shows that things level themselves out over time. Wherever you are in the world, make sure you accept the currency of your clients. The second you add complexity to your client's life, you become a pain to pay.

So you've got a bank account and accept the currency of your client. Job done? Not quite.

Next, give them the option they want to pay you. With large clients, this will be obvious. They pay you via bank transfer so all you need to do is provide your bank details. Unless, of course, you're in a different country. Make it templated on your invoices that you have all your bank account information, including country transfer codes. Sure, not all your customers will need this but a belt and braces approach removes any element of risk.

Is everyone going to pay you via bank transfer? No.

Typically, the larger the organization the longer it is to get on their supplier list. This may take some time in itself. Expect forms and purchase orders. In some cases, maybe even security assessments. When this is the case, think about your fees *before* you start jumping through hoops. I once lost an entire day getting on a supplier's list. But it didn't matter as I'd factored that time into the project.

When you make it to the supplier list, bank transfers are the norm. But there's also going to be the time when someone needs something fast. Certain contacts will have access to a company credit card so they can bypass the supplier list and sign up and execute projects quickly. In these cases, you have two options:

1. Do the work and accept you still need to get on the supplier list and you won't be paid for months.
2. Accept credit card payments.

I know, I know. That means you'll lose about 3% on all your invoices.

Well, only if you don't add that transaction fee to your invoice. It really is as simple as that. In most cases, you can literally add this on and nobody will mention it.

The alternative, and the one I go with, is to say "Sure, you can pay by credit card. There'll be a small charge on the invoice that reflects that." I have a 100% payment rate when including this.

And how about small businesses or startups? No long supplier list sign-up here but also the chance that the money is coming out of an individual's account or a custom fund set aside for marketing.

Payment options like PayPal and cryptocurrency are useful here. You don't need to be a crypto bro to accept cryptocurrency payments, either. If you have a Coinbase (or whatever) account, you can receive payments then transfer them straight to your bank account in your preferred currency.

Being flexible and having different options to receive payment makes you extremely payable. The invoice goes out, the payment arrives. Autonomous.

What should you not do?

Demand payment in a specific currency or format. That's about it. Your inflexibility will cost you in the long run.

In niche cases, your hands may be tied. And I sympathize with you immensely. I know freelancers in Ecuador and Nigeria who find it hard to get paid. PayPal and Coinbase are lifesavers here.

When I send a customer an invoice, they all follow the same template. I literally just select the customer and add the products and services.

Each invoice includes:

- Supplier purchase order number (if they gave you one)
- Supplier address
- Supplier contact
- My contact
- My address
- Product or service
- Number of products or services
- Per item amount
- Total amount
- Invoice number
- Due date
- My payment details
- My overseas payment details
- My company registration number
- Terms for next payment (payment of this invoice confirms you will pay remainder on completion, etc.)

Thanks to the inclusion of these elements, I'm incredibly easy to pay. But what about when you don't get paid?

What to do when you don't get paid

In the spirit of autonomy, automate this process. With invoicing software, like FreeAgent, you can set up auto-reminders when an invoice becomes overdue.

This simple one-time setting, coupled with a watertight contract (see previous chapter), means you forget about chasing up late customers and focus on your craft.

I see zero arguments against using this.

I know a ton of freelancers who spend far too much time asking for their overdue invoices to eventually be paid. I've had literal fights on Twitter with freelancers who complain they don't have time but refuse to be anything but moneylenders to their clients.

Newsflash: you don't have to be nice here. You're a business.

What if they still don't pay?

I really hope you're never in this situation. I haven't been myself. But I wanted to include an example of someone who did, and how they remedied their problem. So I reached out on Twitter for examples and it turns out *every* example was the situation where they didn't have a contract in place.

If you take the scenario of working with a contract versus without a contract, the narrative writes itself.

If you do somehow find yourself not getting paid *even when you have a contract in place*, Sian Lenegan, a business consultant, shared her alligator email with me. Apparently, it worked like a charm!

Hi {Name},

I've been trying to reach you for {x weeks} - wondering if you've been eaten by alligators or you're just plain swamped?

We did a lot of {work/deliverables} for {company/project} and we've provided all the {deliverables}, we were promised payment in return for that output but the money hasn't materialized. Please pick one of the responses and let me know which it is.

a) You have been eaten by alligators

b) You haven't been eaten by alligators but you're ignoring my emails and texts because you owe me money

c) It's something else and you've been meaning to catch up with me but you've been busy fighting alligators, I will let you know by next week what the situation is and make a payment plan so we can sort this out

d) I'm so sorry, complete oversight and I'm sending you {$0000} right now

Please let me know if it's a, b, c or d so that we can both just crack on with our businesses and I don't need to make up any more crazy emails about alligators.

Thanks,

{Your name}

PS Sian says, "For added effect use the alligator emoji as the subject line, always gets an open."

So now you've been paid. What should you do with that money?

What happens when you get paid?

When you're a freelancer, you're not just responsible for your deliverables and sales, you're also responsible for your payroll. People usually react to these things in two ways. They either think this is great because they get all the money and spend little on outgoings. Or they fear messing up because numbers are alien to them. I also hear horror stories (to me at least) about people spending entire days working on payroll and accounts. The notion that someone is doing this fries my mind. I estimate I spend ten minutes per week on my finances.

I split my finance tasks into two segments: when I get paid and when I spend money.

Here's my exact process when I receive payment from a client:

1. Money comes into business bank account.
2. Move 43% of that amount to my **Tax Pot**.

This way, I know that my balance is my genuine spendable business income. The tax pot is exactly that. In reality, I don't pay 43%. That is, however, the amount I was paying when I was employed. So, as a backstop and a nice bonus, I move 43% to the tax pot so I'm covered for all eventualities. When tax-paying season comes around, I make a single payment safe in the knowledge that it's all available. Whatever's left in the tax pot after I've paid tax can either stay there as a buffer or be moved to the main balance.

That's it. I'll match up money with relevant invoices by clicking "approve" when I log into my accounting software every few weeks or so. That keeps my accountant happy.

There are some circumstances when I move money back from the tax pot:

1. Salary
2. Pension
3. Expenses

Each month, pay your own salary. Make it the bare minimum for tax efficiency. In the UK, this is £758.33 (as of January 2023). By doing this, your company is paying you a salary small enough not to be taxed in your personal self-assessment. On paper, this doesn't sound livable. And it's not. So let's become tax-efficient…

Being savvy with your expenses and knowing what you can claim as a legitimate business expense pays for itself here.

These include:

- Working from home expenses (heating, electricity, furniture).
- Travel and hotel costs.
- Entertaining expenses.
- Mileage, petrol, and vehicles.

These are all pretty standard guidelines. But, until you learn exactly what you can spend (and claim as a tax-deductible expense), it's just words on a page.

Here's what you can (and should) claim as a business expense. Note, these are applicable in the UK for limited companies. Always check with your/an accountant first.

Accounting: you can claim for your own time spent on accounting if you don't have an accountant. If you have an accountant, you can claim for their fee.

Advertising & marketing: if you run a campaign to generate new leads, you can claim for the cost of the platform and resources you use.

Business account payments: if you have to pay a fee for your business bank account, or need to pay interest, you can claim for this.

Broadband/internet: claim back the percentage of your home broadband bill you use for business. E.g., if you work 8 hours a day, claim for 33% of your broadband bills.

Business use of home: as above, claim the 33% of your heating, electricity, gas, logs if you work 8 hours per day.

Charity donations: any donation using Gift Aid is applicable for tax relief.

Computer equipment: this covers a wide variety of things you will likely use in your business and personal life. Laptops, printers, cables, chargers, etc. are all covered in this category. The same applies to software and subscriptions used for business.

Equipment your company buys from you as a person: (taken from Freeagent's "Business Costs Expenses for Limited Companies Guide"): If you already own a computer, office chair etc. and want to bring it into your business, you can claim tax relief for its market value at the point you brought it into the business. Check eBay for similar items and then include that cost in the company's accounts. Don't forget that if you are going to carry on using the equipment privately too, HMRC would consider this to be a taxable benefit.

Travel: if you need to *fly, drive, cab, train,* or something more inventive to see a client or attend a business function, you can claim the full amount of this. The same applies to where you are staying. Check your local rules on claiming fuel for mileage if you drive. If you have a company car, even as the sole employee, all mileage is included as the vehicle is a company asset.

Company car: if you have a company car, everything associated with this vehicle is a business expense, with the exception of parking and speeding fines.

Food while traveling: in the above situations when you're traveling, you can claim for food away from your office. These will match up with your dates for other travel expenses.

Swag: if you create merchandise with your name on it to send to prospects and customers, you can claim for this.

Mobile phone: switch your mobile phone contract to a business account in your business name and you can claim the full amount as a business expense.

Pension contributions: you can claim the full amount of every pension contribution. More on pensions in the next section.

Stationery: any pens, notepads, etc. can be claimed as a business expense.

Training: if you sign up for courses or resources to be used exclusively for business purposes, you can claim the full amount of these.

I suggest you take a photo of the section above and stick it to your corkboard above your workstation ready for when you do your accounts. Every element here contributes to a much nicer tax bill at the end of the year and helps reduce the burden on your personal salary.

In the likely event that you are still lacking funds in your personal bank account, there are scenarios where you can make tax-free transfers from your business account to your personal account. These include things like taking dividends from your company. Here, check with local rules. In the UK in 2023, this is capped at £1,000. In 2024, it is being reduced to £500.

If you're desperate for cash from your business account, consider taking a director's loan. Here, you can take a tax-free loan from your business on the basis that you must pay it back.

Outside of these tax efficiencies, it's time to start paying tax. However, running a company means you pay tax for the company and on your reduced "earnings" you withdraw from it. This is a far more efficient way to be a freelancer than working as a sole trader. There is a small caveat that this is only effective at a certain threshold. No accountant or financial advisor wants to commit to confirming what that threshold is. My personal experience says that it's 100% before you start earning £100,000 per year. I paid *a lot* of tax in my first full year as a freelancer and learned the hard way.

In reality, the threshold is based on your profit and loss. I've searched far and wide for the magic number but the best guidance is this...

Okay, it's not easy. I started writing this section out but ended up making it more complicated.

Here's the guidance taken directly from Tuchbands' article, How to become a limited company:

Why a low income businesses should become a limited company

A sole trader with a profit below the personal allowance and the Class 4 National Insurance lower limit will not be liable to pay any tax, but if they earn above the small earnings exception (£6,025 for 2017/18 and £5,065 for 2016-17), then they will be liable to pay Class 2 NI contributions.

If that same person had operated through a limited company and withdrawn the same profit solely through a salary – and not via a dividend – they would not have to pay tax or NI contributions. At a salary level above the lower earnings limit, they would also retain any contribution record for state pension and benefit purposes.

Why a high income businesses should become a limited company

A sole trader who makes a profit of £50,000 would benefit from part of the profit being non-taxable, due to the specifications of their personal allowance. The remainder of the profit would be taxable at the basic rate of income tax and part at the higher rate of income tax. Class 2 and Class 4 National Insurance Contributions would also apply.

If an incorporated business made the same profit of £50,000, the business owner would receive a small salary of less than the current personal allowance and would still receive the remainder of the profit as dividends.

For the 2017/2018 tax year, corporation tax, income tax and employee NICs would amount to £10,076 on profits of £50,000, leaving the owner of the limited company £2,187 better off than a sole trader with the same level of profits.

If the same owner had taken a lower dividend below the basic rate limit and left some profit in the company then they could have paid less tax."

If, at this point, you're still stuck, I strongly advise seeking the advice of an accountant or financial advisor.

It's through my financial advisor that I have, without any real financial knowledge, accrued a pension pot of £70,000 and an accessible ISA of £30,000 on top of my regular income by the time I am 30. And all without feeling like I'm missing out on disposable personal income. I live a very good life balanced somewhere between saving up for the long term and "I'm here for a good time not a long time".

Some freelancers report they miss the employer benefits like pensions.

"As a freelancer for over 15 years, I certainly feel that freedom was oversold though. It has probably also cost me about $250k in employee benefits, especially pension controls too."

These are the thoughts of a disgruntled freelancer who didn't take any steps to protect or invest in their future finances. And I can only blame the individual. When you become a freelancer, you are responsible for *all* aspects of your business. And that includes pensions and benefits.

- Do I miss having a 3% pension match from my previous employer? Absolutely not.
- Do I miss discounted dental, and a health policy never used? Nope.
- Do I miss any employer benefits? Not even slightly.

I do, however, understand the hesitation to lose these things. What if I suddenly need access to something my employer *did* provide? I'd feel like an idiot. But that's the bullet you bite. And after your likely rise in rate, you won't even notice it anyway.

I haven't ever come across anything I've ever needed or missed in the traditional benefits package. My pension works harder in an investment portfolio, I have my own life insurance, I should get around to making a will*, and I recently paid for my dental treatment upfront.

*I made one after writing this section. It took less than 30 minutes on farewill.com

Sure, I could have got some of these if I stayed with a company long enough. But, when weighed up against my potential earnings and freedom as a freelancer, there is no doubt in my mind I am better off both financially and mentally.

But only because of the autonomy I've created for myself.

CHAPTER 8

HOW TO DIVERSIFY INCOME WITHOUT REINVENTING THE WHEEL

For the longest time, people told me "you should make a course". I had no interest in doing this because I loved writing. I didn't want to "make a course". But today I have three products that supplement my writing and strategy income:

1. $99 Blogging Course
2. $35 Content Promotion Checklist
3. $25 Book

If I sell one of each per week, that's an extra $8,000 in my bank account every year.

And getting to this stage was fairly easy. Because I was creating products based on my expertise. My blogging course is literally me recording a typical day-in-the-life, my content promotion checklist is a product I use myself every day, and my book is recounting things I've learned first-hand. These were all fairly low effort compared to coming up with a brand new idea. And they're all things people need or want. There is both demand and the ability to execute. So I quickly realized it made sense to diversify my income without taking too much of a leap away from my areas of expertise.

I can talk about creating these three things, and I will expand on the *how* in a few sentences. Outside of courses, checklists, and books, also consider creating:

- Affiliate marketing (taking a commission when referring products)
- Sell something related to your hobby (like arts and crafts)
- Ad revenue on personal/niche sites
- Webinar appearances
- Consultation hours
- YouTube videos
- Selling designs
- Brand deals
- Newsletter
- Podcasts
- Coaching

When I asked my Twitter audience for other ways freelancers can diversify their income, one of the best answers I got (and was hoping for) was this from Sebastian Tigerschiöld, a freelance web developer:

"Add a proximity service. For web dev, add hosting, SEO, marketing, email setup, etc."

If you recall what Brooklin Nash said in the blog post I shared earlier in the book, "The biggest jump in my income came when I started helping clients with earlier stages of content strategy and planning."

For me, it was the other way around this year. Here's a breakdown of my income for January to November 2022:

- Content marketing retainers: $78,500
- Blog posts/eBooks: $100,000
- Affiliate sales: $800
- Products: $2,500
- SEO: $2,500

If I'd never taken the step out of content creation (executing someone else's strategy), I'd be missing the skills to charge for additional retainers like content strategy and SEO consultancy.

On the face of it, it probably means I'd be writing more blog posts. Which, as you can see, pays the bills. But consistently doing the same thing (typing) can wear you out—and that's coming from someone who writes for fun outside of work too.

So, let's put this into action. It's one thing saying you should expand your skill set. But how do you get started?

How to create an online course

I've written a blog post covering how I created my online course. I've included that in this section.

How To Record Online Course Videos

Recording your first online course video can be a daunting task.

If you've never used video or never created educational materials before, starting from scratch can feel like getting dressed in the dark.

How do I know this?

Because I was in the same position about 18 months ago.

Fast forward those 18 months and I've made thousands in online course sales, have many videos on YouTube, and use videos with almost all my customers.

In this post, I'm going to share how I recorded my first online course video and throw in some bonus tips for creation and promotion.

1 - Prepping your online course

There are three key areas to consider when preparing your online course:

- What are you going to record?
- Are you going to make money from your online course?
- How are you going to record your online course video?

What are you going to record?

For the "what", think about your core online course content.

You might be creating an online course video to help other copywriters conquer writer's block.

It might be a video course on how to gain more social media followers.

Or it could be something super-specific to your set of niche skills, like knitting or football analysis.

When you know your topic, it's time to think about the format. Formats include:

- Live demos
- End-to-end walkthroughs
- Q&As
- Simply talking to the camera
- Presentations with slides
- A mixture of all the above

Judging what your audience wants rather than what you'd like to do is key here. If you don't think about your audience, they will lose focus and you stand less of a chance of them referring to their peers.

So now you know what your course is going to be about and how you're going to structure it.

Before you dive in and start recording, what is your goal for this course?

If it's to grow your personal brand or grow a community, it needs to be high-quality.

If people are parting with their money at any point, it also needs to be high-quality.

If you don't want to charge for your online course video, there are still other ways to make money.

How do you monetize a video course?

In the preparation phase, think about whether and how you're going to make money from your video course.

Even if you don't plan to charge a fee, stick around in this section as you could be leaving money on the table.

Here are 10 ways to monetize a video course:

1. Charge a one-off fee
2. Charge a recurring fee
3. Find a sponsor
4. Use affiliate links
5. Create your own affiliate program
6. Monetize your YouTube channel
7. Promote your other products
8. Promote your other services
9. Embed your course to your blog and turn on AdSense
10. Add a tipping service like Buy Me A Coffee

If you intend on charging for your course, platforms like Gumroad and Udemy offer easy upload processes.

Spend some time getting to know each platform. They have different payout methods and different in-platform sharing options.

How are you going to record your online course video?

For the "how", the first thing to need to assess is your equipment setup.

The basics you'll need include: a webcam or DSLR camera, a microphone, and lighting. Let's assume you've already got a laptop or PC at this point.

You could spend ages researching which webcams YouTubers use or you could opt for something that will get the job done.

Unless you're aiming for seriously high production, the Logitech Brio paired with an Elgato Key Light Air is a solid combination for recording online course videos.

The most important element when creating an online course video is your audio.

Viewers are forgiving of less-than-perfect camera quality and lighting if they can hear you.

Having been through many microphones, I've landed on the Shure MV7. It's far superior to anything else in its price bracket.

The final piece of equipment you may need is a laptop stand. When recording your online course videos, think about the camera position and what you want the viewer to see.

In the image below, you can see I recycled my unused jewelry box instead. I pop my laptop on top when I need to record.

While this setup doesn't look particularly Hollywood, it falls within budget and ticks all the boxes for great quality online course videos.

2 - Recording your online course videos

Now it's time to get recording.

The missing piece of the puzzle is your video recorder.

Head to tella.tv and start recording videos straight from your browser.

With Tella, you can record your screen and webcam simultaneously, so you don't need to stitch elements together after recording.

It's also free for your first 10 videos and there's no limit on screen recording time.

When you sign up to Tella (in just four clicks), you can start recording straight away. There's nothing to install and nothing to configure.

At this point, the blog goes into detail about Tella. I didn't want to include that in this book, but I do think it's the best choice for recording videos for online courses.

When you're happy with your final product, you might think that it's the end of the process.

It's only the end if you don't want anybody to watch it.

Next, let's dig into 10 platforms to share your online course and learn how to hyper-utilize them.

3 - How to sell video courses online

What we're not going to do here is simply share your course on social media.

Sure, social media plays a big part in video distribution. But we're going to focus on finding the right places to promote your online course. And once we've found them, we're going the extra mile to use all the free functionality available.

How do I sell a course on the internet?

Selling online products means you need to get in front of the right people online.

Let's walk through which platforms to use and how best to use them.

1 - Twitter

We all know how to send a tweet. But few people spend enough time planning their tweets.

Things to consider when promoting your online course on Twitter include:

- Timing: when is your audience engaged?
- Imagery: what does your audience respond to?
- Pricing: what's affordable for your followers?

Outside of the promotional tweets, consider the build-up to launching your course.

If you talk about a product and get people's opinions while you're making it, you stand a better chance of turning those people into buyers.

In contrast, a tweet out of the blue asking for payment rarely works.

On Twitter, you're not limited to single tweets either.

You can craft viral Twitter threads and include a link to your online course. Of course, these take time to get right. But, like most things with marketing, the time you put in is often retrieved in your sales figures.

Don't limit yourself to your own tweets, either. When other people tweet about the topic you've created your online course video on, engage with them.

Not every reply needs to be "Hey, buy my course!" but making people aware you're a subject matter expert means they might follow you then see you have a course later on.

2 - LinkedIn

A lot of the same tactics you use on Twitter apply on LinkedIn too.

Understanding when your audience is online and what they respond to are musts.

Also like Twitter, there are other ways to gain more eyeballs on your online course.

Finding LinkedIn Groups associated with your course content opens the door to an engaged pool of LinkedIn users looking for content and help on your topic of expertise.

Again, a blatant sales post may not gain many sales. Engaging and demonstrating your authority will.

To find LinkedIn Groups relevant to your course content, search your topic and filter to "Groups".

3 - Facebook

On Facebook, you've likely got connections who know you. They might be old school friends, family members, or people you've met online.

The simple act of knowing you means they might like to support you if they are also interested in your video course content.

Rather than just gambling on people being nice, Facebook is another open door to groups with engaged users.

Like LinkedIn Groups, Facebook has functionality where like-minded people can hang out and discuss niche topics.

To infiltrate these communities, you must gain trust rather than arrive and start spamming everyone.

④ - Blogs

When you write high-quality blogs that rank high on Google, you stand a great chance of being found by people with specific search intent.

This means when people search for something and you answer their questions, they are likely to invest in your product to become an expert too.

This is the tactic employed by content marketing teams in both B2B and B2C. By giving away something for free (your blog content), you are more likely to receive an exchange for a paid product.

But only if your content is high-quality.

When you've built trust in your blog post, find the right time to add a call to action.

It might be right at the end of your post. But it might also be more relevant at certain action points.

⑤ - Gumroad Discover

When people have started to download your online products, the platform you host them on could recognize it's selling well.

In this case, platforms (like Gumroad) want to showcase their best creators so both parties make money.

There's no shortcut to being featured by these platforms. But you can optimize your online course using tags, categories, and displaying ratings from existing customers.

6 - Affiliates

On most online course platforms, you can create affiliate links for bloggers, influencers, and happy customers to use.

Here, they get a % (that you choose) when they refer someone with their unique link.

Pro tip: offer a higher % commission on the first five sales to encourage new affiliates to push your online course.

7 - Community

In Slack communities or any online area with an engaged audience, you've got an audience with a common interest.

You can penetrate these communities by becoming a regular contributor or a sponsor.

Regular helpful contributions build trust and open the door to letting someone know you have a course on that exact topic.

Becoming a sponsor shortcuts that but has the negatives of 1) costing money and 2) being a cold introduction without building trust.

8 - Podcasts

In the same way, you can sponsor a community, you can also sponsor a podcast.

The key here is finding the right podcast. Advertising on any old podcast might get tons of listeners but the chance of them needing your online course doesn't correlate.

Identify podcasts with similar interests to your course and create customized promo codes so the podcast gets something out of it too.

Some may charge a fee, or some prefer an affiliate relationship.

9 - Influencers

Like communities and podcasts, using "influencers" is tapping into existing audiences.

People with a large number of followers or highly-engaged niche viewers take a small cut of the money you make (affiliate) or may ask for a fee in exchange for promoting.

To find the right influencers to collaborate with, check engagement stats like likes, comments, and shares as well as the number of followers.

Thousands of followers are worthless if none are engaged.

Send a DM or email to influencers you identify explaining why you think your online course is relevant to their audience. Don't forget to include what's in it for them.

10 - Email

Rather than trying to creep into other people's audiences, why not use your own audience?

If you run an email newsletter or have email addresses from selling other products, send a one-time, time-based email offering a small discount for early buyers of your online course video.

When launching my second independent product, the majority of people who bought my first online course video made another purchase.

Offering a loyalty discount is a surefire way to lure people in if they enjoyed your first product.

So, there we have it! You've successfully learned how to plan, record, monetize, and promote your online course.

How to create checklists and templates

Creating checklists and templates is easy. I literally started with a Google Sheet, added some lines with things to work through, then added the how, the suggested tool to use, and an example in the wild. I then repurposed this to an Excel version and a Notion version. My checklist has 50 places you can promote your content and costs $39. That's tremendous value if you don't already have a process for content distribution.

The challenge around creating checklists and templates like this is finding a market. There's little point investing time into a product if there's no demand.

In my case, I saw everyone on Twitter, in LinkedIn groups, and on webinars complaining they didn't know how to find new places to promote their content. So, I fixed that problem for them. I've sold 121 this year and it took me less than a day to create.

How to write a book

This section isn't going to be a book publishing process. But I'd like to point out (and reinforce something covered in the finding a niche section) how you can start writing a book without creating a monumental (and not very autonomous) pile of work for yourself.

In this book, I've done three things:

1. Recall personal experiences
2. Outreach to my immediate network
3. Repurpose existing content I've created

By relying on my personal experience, I've almost eradicated the research process that is so time-consuming when starting to write a book or a blog post about a technical topic.

By having already built a social network (see chapter on sharing content and networking), I can post a tweet or LinkedIn message and get responses within hours. These all help me add different perspectives so it's not all me me me.

By repurposing existing content, I make the job shorter by a number of days. I tend to write in batches of 1,500 words. I've included several blog posts and Twitter threads in this book which make the overall time to execute much shorter. And this comes with the benefit of already being strength-tested. People paid me to write this content or it got a great reaction.

With any product you create to diversify your income, the most important thing to remember is the same thing you should remember when trying to dominate a niche as a freelancer. I'll repeat it word for word so it one day becomes ingrained in your brain.

My biggest advice to freelancers looking to find their niche is:

Write about what you know.

HOW TO BECOME AN AUTONOMOUS FREELANCER RIGHT NOW

We've covered a lot in this book. I wanted to share my (freelance) life's work so people like you can happily and productively build a successful freelance career.

I've seen and heard too many freelancers who either don't make money, are burnt out, or spend far too much time on tasks that add zero value. All the while, I've had the greatest 5 years of my life, earning money I thought I could only make if I one day become a corporate CEO.

Instead, I go to the beach every day. I finish up around 2pm. I have every Friday off. I spend time on passion projects. I mentor other freelancers. My work-life balance is swayed heavily towards life.

And I'd love for you to get here too.

So, where to start first?

The first thing that changed my life was working on my own terms. Saying no to customers I didn't want, saying yes to working when I am productive, and cutting out activities that added zero value (monetary or otherwise) created this flow state where my craft became autonomous. It's like recalling muscle memory and getting a task done without distractions, pressure, or stress. I am totally self-governed because I have set the deliverables, the timelines, and the costs.

Take this away as the first thing you do. And if you do nothing else but this, consider it a win.

Write down (with a pen and paper) your perfect work day.

That's it. That's the first step you're going to take. Everything else in your freelance future depends on this.

Thanks for reading my book. I genuinely hope and have complete faith that I've created something helpful and actionable for junior and seasoned freelancers who realize they can make (even small) changes that bring big results.

If you enjoyed this book, follow me on Twitter @DomKent

TOOLS AND RESOURCES CALLED OUT IN THIS BOOK

Here's everything I listed as a useful tool to at least try as you strive to achieve freelance autonomy:

1. Hypefury (social media scheduling)
2. Typefully (Twitter thread creation)
3. PayPal (receiving payments abroad)
4. Coinbase (receiving payments abroad)
5. BuyMeACoffee (monetizing videos and courses)
6. Tella (recording videos)
7. The Four-Hour Work Week (book on working less)
8. Drive (book on what motivates us)
9. The Chimp Paradox (book on mind management)
10. Atomic Habits (book on forming habits)
11. My content promotion checklist
12. My blogging course
13. Freelance contract template (free)

(If you click these links on the ebook version of this book, I'll get a small kickback for referring you. Remember the chapter on diversifying your income?)

Thanks again. Happy freelancing.

www.ingramcontent.com/pod-product-compliance
Lightning Source LLC
Chambersburg PA
CBHW052356220526
45465CB00003BB/1131